THE UK TOWER FRYER COOKBOOK FOR BEGINNERS

1000 Days Simple and Tasty Recipes for Effortless Cooking at Home, with Expert Tips

to Build Your Confidence in the Kitchen|Full Color Pictures Version

TESSA D. MILLER

EDITOR: LYN   INTERIOR DESIGN: FAIZAN

COVER ART: ABR   FOOD STYLIST: JO

Table of Contents

Introduction

If you're looking for a healthier way to enjoy your favorite fried foods, then the Tower Air Fryer is the perfect appliance for you. Unlike traditional deep frying, which requires a lot of oil and can be messy and time-consuming, the Tower Air Fryer uses hot air to cook your food, resulting in crispy, delicious meals without the extra calories and fat. with a range of temperature settings and a timer for precise cooking, you can easily customize the cooking process to achieve the perfect results every time. Whether you're cooking up a quick breakfast, making a tasty appetizer, or preparing a full-course meal for your family, the Tower Air Fryer makes it easy to cook healthy, flavorful meals that you'll love. So why not give it a try and see for yourself how the Tower Air Fryer can transform your cooking and your health!

The Tower Air Fryer is a revolutionary kitchen appliance that uses hot air to cook food, providing a healthier alternative to traditional frying methods. It allows you to enjoy the taste and texture of fried food with little to no oil, making it a great option for those who want to eat healthier or reduce their calorie intake. with adjustable temperature control and a timer for precise cooking, the Tower Air Fryer is versatile and easy to use. Whether you're cooking breakfast, lunch, or dinner, the Tower Air Fryer can help you create delicious, crispy meals with minimal effort.

What is a Tower Air Fryer?

A Tower Air Fryer is a kitchen appliance that uses hot air to cook food, providing a healthier alternative to traditional frying methods. It works by circulating hot air around the food, cooking it to a crispy texture without the need for added oil. The Tower Air Fryer typically has adjustable temperature control and a timer for precise cooking, making it easy to cook a variety of foods such as chicken, fish, vegetables, and even desserts. It is versatile and easy to use, making it a popular choice for those who want to enjoy fried food without the extra calories and fat. with its compact size and ease of use, the Tower Air Fryer is a great addition to any kitchen.

Explanation of How it Works

The Tower Air Fryer works by using a convection mechanism to circulate hot air around the food. When you turn on the appliance and set the temperature, the heating element inside the air fryer heats the air to the desired temperature. The hot air then circulates around the food, cooking it to a crispy texture. The air fryer is designed with a basket or tray where you can place the food you want to cook, allowing the hot air to circulate evenly and cook the food from all sides.

The Tower Air Fryer is particularly effective at cooking foods that are traditionally fried, such as French fries, chicken wings, and onion rings. Since it uses hot air instead of oil, it can cook these foods to a crispy texture without the added calories and fat. Some air fryers also come with accessories such as baking pans or skewers, allowing you to cook a variety of foods in different ways.

One of the main benefits of the Tower Air Fryer is that it can cook food to a crispy texture without the need for added oil. For example, you can cook French fries in the air fryer by simply cutting the potatoes into strips and placing them in the basket. The hot air circulates around the fries, cooking them to a crispy texture on the outside while keeping them tender on the inside.

Another popular use for the Tower Air Fryer is cooking chicken wings. Instead of deep frying the wings in oil, you can season them with your favorite spices and place them in the air fryer basket. The hot air circulates around the wings, cooking them to a crispy texture while keeping the meat juicy and flavorful.

In addition to fried foods, the Tower Air Fryer can also be used to cook a variety of other dishes, including roasted vegetables, grilled cheese sandwiches, and even desserts like apple fritters. The adjustable temperature control and timer make it easy to customize the cooking process for different types of foods.

Benefits of Using An Air Fryer

CONSISTENT COOKING

Air fryers use circulating hot air to cook food evenly on all sides, resulting in consistent and predictable results. This can be especially helpful for novice cooks who may struggle with getting the right temperature or cook time.

This cooking method is known as "rapid air technology," and it works by using high-powered fans to circulate hot air around the food. The hot air is generated by a heating element located above the food basket, and it circulates at a high speed, ensuring that the food is cooked quickly and e

VENLY.

This even cooking is one of the main benefits of using an air fryer. It ensures that the food is cooked thoroughly, with a crispy exterior and a moist interior. It also eliminates the need to turn the food over, which is often required when using traditional cooking methods.

SAFETY

Air fryers are a safer option than traditional deep fryers, as there is no risk of hot oil splashing or spills. Additionally, many air fryers come with safety features such as automatic shut-off or cool-touch handles to prevent accidents.

Another safety benefit of air fryers is that they are designed to be used indoors, while traditional deep fryers are typically used outdoors or in commercial kitchens. Using an air fryer inside your home eliminates the risk of outdoor hazards, such as propane tanks or open flames.

CONVENIENCE

Air fryers are designed to be easy to use and require minimal cleanup. Many models come with removable parts that can be washed in the dishwasher, making cleanup a breeze. This convenience factor can be especially helpful for busy individuals or families who don't have a lot of time to spend in the kitchen. Unlike deep fryers, which can be messy and require a lot of oil, air fryers use minimal oil or no oil at all. This means that there is no need to deal with hot oil spills, which can be dangerous and difficult to clean up.

Most air fryer models have simple controls and are easy to operate. Many have pre-programmed settings for popular foods like chicken, fish, and french fries, making it easy to cook these foods with the touch of a button.

In terms of cleanup, air fryers have removable and dishwasher-safe parts, making them easy to clean. Most models have a non-stick coating that prevents food from sticking, and any residue can be wiped away with a damp cloth or sponge.

VERSATILITY

Air fryers can be used to cook a wide variety of foods, from crispy chicken wings to tender vegetables. Air fryers are versatile kitchen appliances that can be used to cook a wide variety of foods. They are not limited to frying or cooking certain types of food; instead, they can be used to cook a variety of meals.

Air fryers can be used to cook chicken, fish, vegetables, potatoes, french fries, onion rings, and even desserts like cakes and cookies. They can also be used to reheat leftovers, toast bread, and roast nuts.

In fact, many air fryer models come with a recipe book that includes a variety of recipes for breakfast, lunch, and dinner. The possibilities are endless with an air fryer, and you can experiment with different foods and cooking techniques to find what works best for you.

It's worth noting that while air fryers can cook a wide variety of foods, it's important to follow the manufacturer's instructions and recommended cooking times for each food item to achieve the best results.

QUICK COOKING

Air fryers cook food quickly, often in just a fraction of the time it would take to cook the same food in an oven or on a stovetop. This makes them a great option for weeknight dinners or when you're short on time. Plus, the quick cooking time can help lock in moisture and flavor, resulting in tasty, succulent dishes. air fryers are known for cooking food quickly. They use a high-powered fan to circulate hot air around the food, which helps to cook it quickly and evenly.

The hot air generated by the air fryer can reach temperatures of up to 400°F (200°C), which is much hotter than a conventional oven. This high temperature allows food to cook faster, reducing the overall cooking time.

In addition to the high temperature, the circulating hot air ensures that the food is cooked evenly on all sides, resulting in a crispy exterior and a moist interior. This is especially beneficial when cooking foods that typically take a long time to cook, such as chicken or fish.

ENERGY EFFICIENCY

Compared to traditional ovens, air fryers can be considered more energy-efficient. This is because they use a smaller space to cook food, and they heat up faster, which means they require less energy to operate. Air fryers use less energy than traditional ovens or deep fryers, making them a more eco-friendly option for cooking. This can help reduce your energy bill and lower your carbon footprint, all while enjoying delicious meals.

HEALTHIER COOKING

Air fryers use hot air to cook food, which means that they require little to no oil. This can lead to a reduction in the amount of calories and fat in your meals, which can be beneficial for individuals who are trying to manage their weight or reduce their risk of obesity. By using an air fryer, you can still enjoy your favorite fried foods, but with fewer calories and less fat. However, it's important to note that the calorie and fat content of your meals will depend on the specific ingredients you use and how you prepare them, so it's always a good idea to consult with a healthcare professional or registered dietitian before making any significant changes to your diet.

Chapter 2
Mastering the Tower Air Fryer

How to Use the Air Fryer

THE BASIC FUNCTIONS OF A TOWER AIR FRYER INCLUDE:
1. Frying: The primary function of an air fryer is to fry food using hot air. Tower air fryers use a rapid air circulation technology to circulate hot air around the food, resulting in crispy, evenly cooked food.
2. Roasting: Some tower air fryers have a roasting function that allows you to roast meats and vegetables. This function typically uses a lower temperature than the frying function and takes longer to cook the food.
3. Baking: Some tower air fryers have a baking function that allows you to bake small cakes, muffins, and other baked goods. This function typically uses a lower temperature and longer cooking time than the frying function.
4. Grilling: Some tower air fryers have a grilling function that allows you to grill meats, fish, and vegetables. This function typically uses a higher temperature and takes less time than the roasting function.
5. Reheating: Tower air fryers can also be used to reheat leftover food. This function typically uses a lower temperature and shorter cooking time than the frying function.
6. Defrosting: Some tower air fryers have a defrosting function that allows you to defrost frozen food quickly and easily.

THE CONTROLS OF A TOWER AIR FRYER:

1. Power button: The power button is used to turn the air fryer on and off.
2. Temperature control: The temperature control allows you to adjust the cooking temperature. The temperature can usually be adjusted in increments of 10 degrees, and the temperature range is typically between 180°C to 200°C (or 356°F to 392°F).
3. Timer control: The timer control allows you to set the cooking time for your food. The cooking time can usually be set in increments of 1 minute, and the maximum cooking time is typically around 60 minutes.
4. Preset programs: Some tower air fryers come with preset programs for popular foods like chicken, fish, and french fries. These programs automatically set the temperature and cooking time for the selected food, making it easier to cook your favorite meals with the touch of a button.
5. Start/Stop button: The start/stop button is used to begin or end the cooking process.
6. Display: Most tower air fryers have a digital display that shows the cooking time, temperature, and other settings. Some models also have an LED display that shows the cooking progress.
7. Food basket release button: The food basket release button is used to remove the food basket from the air fryer. This button is usually located on the handle of the food basket.
8. Food basket: The food basket is where you place the food for cooking. It is usually removable and dishwasher-safe for easy cleaning.
9. Air inlet: The air inlet is located at the back of the air fryer and allows air to enter the appliance to circulate around the food.

Tips for Perfect Air Frying

SHAKE THE BASKET FREQUENTLY.

Shaking the basket frequently during cooking is a great tip for achieving even cooking and crispy results in your air fryer. By shaking the basket, you can help ensure that all sides of the food are exposed to the hot air, preventing any sticking or clumping of food and promoting even browning. Depending on the type of food you're cooking, it's generally a good idea to shake the basket every 5-10 minutes to ensure even cooking. Just be sure to use oven mitts or tongs to safely remove the basket from the air fryer before shaking it.

CHECK THE TEMPERATURE AND TIME.

Checking the temperature and time are both important for achieving optimal cooking results in your air fryer. Most air fryers come with a temperature control and timer, which you can set according to the recipe you're following or based on your personal preferences.

It's a good idea to preheat the air fryer for a few minutes before adding your food, and then use a thermometer to check the internal temperature of the food as it cooks. This can help ensure that your food is fully cooked and safe to eat.

Similarly, checking the time is important to prevent overcooking or undercooking your food. Depending on the type of food you're cooking, the cooking time may vary. It's important to follow the recipe instructions or use a timer to avoid any guesswork.

By checking the temperature and time, you can ensure that your food is cooked to perfection every time, with the right level of crispiness and doneness.

USE YOUR AIR FRYER TO HEAT FROZEN FOODS.

You can use your air fryer to heat up frozen foods, and it's actually a great way to achieve crispy results while avoiding the need for a deep fryer or oven.

To heat up frozen foods in your air fryer, simply preheat the air fryer to the recommended temperature, and then place the frozen food in the basket. Cook for the recommended time and shake the basket occasionally to ensure even cooking.

Frozen foods that can be cooked in an air fryer include french fries, chicken wings, onion rings, mozzarella sticks, and more. Just be sure to check the package instructions for cooking times and temperatures.

Using your air fryer to heat up frozen foods is a quick and easy way to enjoy crispy and delicious snacks and meals, without the need for extra oil or equipment. Plus, it can be a healthier alternative to deep frying or oven baking.

DON'T OVERCROWD THE AIR FRYER BASKET.

It's important to avoid overcrowding the air fryer basket when cooking, as this can prevent air from circulating properly and result in unevenly cooked food.

When cooking with an air fryer, it's best to leave some space between the food items in the basket to allow for proper air circulation. This will help ensure that the food cooks evenly and achieves the desired level of crispiness.

If you need to cook a large amount of food, it's better to cook it in multiple batches instead of trying to cram everything into the basket at once. This will help ensure that the food cooks properly and tastes its best.

By avoiding overcrowding the air fryer basket, you can achieve crispy and evenly cooked food every time, with the perfect texture and flavor.

USE ALUMINUM FOIL.

Using aluminum foil in an air fryer can be a helpful trick in certain situations, but it's important to use it correctly to avoid any potential hazards.

Aluminum foil can be used to line the air fryer basket, which can help prevent sticking and make cleanup easier. However, it's important to use only a small amount of foil and to avoid covering the entire basket, as this can block airflow and prevent proper cooking.

It's also important to use heavy-duty aluminum foil, which is more durable and less likely to tear or puncture during cooking. Additionally, be sure to avoid using any aluminum foil that has come into contact with acidic or salty foods, as this can cause corrosion and potentially release harmful substances.

Overall, using aluminum foil in an air fryer can be a helpful tool when used correctly and in moderation. Just be sure to follow safety guidelines and use it only as needed to achieve the desired cooking results.

Safety Tips and Maintenance Tips

SAFETY TIPS:
1. Always read the manufacturer's instructions and safety precautions before using your air fryer.
2. Keep the air fryer away from water and other liquids.
3. Never immerse the air fryer in water or any other liquid.
4. Always use the air fryer on a flat, stable surface.
5. Keep children and pets away from the air fryer during use, as it can get very hot.
6. Do not touch the air fryer basket or any other parts while it is in use, as they can become very hot.
7. Do not use metal utensils or abrasive materials to clean the air fryer, as this can damage the non-stick coating.

MAINTENANCE TIPS:
1. Always unplug the air fryer and let it cool completely before cleaning.
2. Clean the air fryer after each use to prevent buildup of food residue and grease.
3. Use a soft, damp cloth or sponge to clean the air fryer, and avoid using harsh chemicals or abrasive materials.
4. Remove and clean the basket and tray regularly to prevent sticking and maintain optimal cooking results.
5. Check the air fryer heating element and fan regularly for any signs of damage or malfunction.
6. Store the air fryer in a dry, cool place when not in use.

Air Fryer Cooking Chart

Food	Temperature (°C)	Cooking Time (minutes)
French fries (thin)	200	10-15
French fries (thick)	200	15-20
Chicken wings	180	20-25
Chicken breast	180	15-20
Salmon fillet	200	8-10
Shrimp	200	8-10
Onion rings	200	8-10
Vegetables (broccoli, etc.)	180	10-15
Frozen vegetables (mix)	180	10-15
Breaded fish fillets	200	10-12
Hamburgers	200	8-10
Bacon	180	6-8
Sausages	180	12-15
Meatballs	180	12-15
Baked potatoes	200	45-50
Sweet potatoes	200	20-25
Chicken breasts	200	15-20 min
Chicken thighs	200	20-25 min
Chicken wings	200	18-20 min
Fish fillets	200	8-12 min
Shrimp	200	6-8 min
Scallops	200	6-8 min
Salmon	200	10-12 min
Pork chops	200	12-15 min
Pork tenderloin	200	20-25 min
Steak (1 inch thick)	200	8-10 min
Hamburger patties	200	8-10 min
Hot dogs/sausages	200	6-8 min
French fries	200	15-20 min
Sweet potato fries	200	15-20 min
Potato wedges	200	15-20 min

Food	Temperature (°C)	Cooking Time (minutes)
Onion rings	200	12-15 min
Zucchini/squash fries	200	10-12 min
Broccoli/cauliflower	200	8-10 min
Brussel sprouts	200	12-15 min
Carrots	200	12-15 min
Asparagus	200	6-8 min
Corn on the cob	200	12-15 min
Baked potatoes	200	40-45 min
Stuffed mushrooms	200	8-10 min
Roasted peppers	200	8-10 min
Chicken nuggets	200	10-12 min
Meatballs	200	10-12 min
Spring rolls	200	10-12 min
Mozzarella sticks	200	6-8 min
Jalapeno poppers	200	8-10 min
Quiche	180	25-30 min
Puff pastry	200	10-12 min
Apple turnovers	200	12-15 min
Chocolate chip cookies	180	6-8 min

Note: Cooking times may vary depending on the type and brand of air fryer, as well as the size and thickness of the food being cooked. Always refer to the manufacturer's instructions and use a food thermometer to ensure that food is cooked to a safe temperature.

Chapter 3
Breakfast Recipes

Breakfast Potatoes
Prep time: 10 minutes | Cook time:20 minutes |Serves 6

- 1½ teaspoons rapeseed oil, divided, plus more for misting
- 4 large potatoes, skins on, cut into cubes
- 2 teaspoons seasoned salt, divided
- 1 teaspoon minced garlic, divided
- 2 large green or red bell peppers, cut into 2.5cm chunks
- ½ onion, diced

1. Lightly mist the air fryer basket with rapeseed oil.
2. In a medium bowl, toss the potatoes with ½ teaspoon of rapeseed oil. Sprinkle with 1 teaspoon of seasoned salt and ½ teaspoon of minced garlic. Stir to coat.
3. Place the seasoned potatoes in the air fryer basket in a single layer.
4. Cook at 190°C for 5 minutes. Shake the basket and cook for another 5 minutes.
5. Meanwhile, in a medium bowl, toss the bell peppers and onion with the remaining ½ teaspoon of rapeseed oil.
6. Sprinkle the peppers and onions with the remaining 1 teaspoon of seasoned salt and ½ teaspoon of minced garlic. Stir to coat.
7. Add the seasoned peppers and onions to the air fryer basket with the potatoes.
8. Cook for 5 minutes. Shake the basket and cook for an additional 5 minutes.

Strawberries and Cream Baked Oatmeal
Prep time: 10 minutes | Cook time:25 minutes |Serves 2

- 1 cup (170 g) sliced strawberries
- 1 egg
- 3/4 cup (180 ml) milk
- 1/4 cup (60 ml) heavy cream
- 1 cup (80 g) rolled oats
- 2 tablespoons (19 g) brown sugar
- 1/2 teaspoon baking powder
- 1/2 teaspoon cinnamon
- 1/2 teaspoon ginger
- Pinch salt
- 1 tablespoon (14 g) unsalted butter (optional)

1. Place the sliced strawberries in the bottom of the cake pan insert for the air fryer, reserving a few for garnish. In a small bowl, whisk together the egg, milk, and cream and pour it over the strawberries in the pan.
2. In a small bowl, combine the rolled oats, brown sugar, baking powder, spices, and salt. Add the dry ingredients to the wet ingredients in the cake pan and stir to combine. Allow to rest for 10 minutes. Place the reserved strawberries on top of the oatmeal.
3. Place the cake pan in the air fryer and bake at 320°F (160°C) for 15 minutes until the oatmeal is warmed through and puffed. Spoon the oatmeal into bowls. If desired, add a pat of butter to each bowl for extra richness.

Spinach and Mushroom Mini Quiche

Prep time: 10 minutes | Cook time:15 minutes |Serves 4

- 1 teaspoon olive oil, plus more for spraying
- 1 cup coarsely chopped mushrooms
- 1 cup fresh baby spinach, shredded
- 4 eggs, beaten
- ½ cup grated Cheddar cheese
- ½ cup grated mozzarella cheese
- ¼ teaspoon salt
- ¼ teaspoon black pepper

1. Preheat the air fryer to 350°F (180°C).
2. Spray 4 silicone baking cups with olive oil and set aside.
3. In a medium sauté pan over medium heat, warm 1 teaspoon of olive oil. Add the mushrooms and sauté until soft, 3 to 4 minutes.
4. Add the spinach and cook until wilted, 1 to 2 minutes. Set aside.
5. In a medium bowl, whisk together the eggs, Cheddar cheese, mozzarella cheese, salt, and pepper.
6. Gently fold the mushrooms and spinach into the egg mixture.
7. Pour ¼ of the mixture into each silicone baking cup.
8. Place the baking cups into the air fryer basket and air fry for 5 minutes. Stir the mixture in each ramekin slightly and air fry until the egg has set, an additional 3 to 5 minutes. Serve hot.

Southwest Frittata

Prep time: 10 minutes | Cook time: 18 to 20 minutes | Makes 6 slices

- Cooking spray
- 4 eggs
- 4 sausages, fully cooked and chopped
- 1 cup Cheddar-Monterey Jack cheese blend
- ½ cup diced bell pepper
- 1 scallion, finely chopped
- 1 teaspoon hot sauce
- ½ teaspoon salt
- ½ teaspoon ground black pepper
- ¼ teaspoon chili powder

1. Preheat the air fryer. (This will help create a nice crust and decrease the cooking time a bit to keep the frittata from getting too brown on top.)
2. Spray a non-stick 6- or 7-inch baking pan with cooking spray.
3. In a medium bowl, add the eggs, sausages, cheese, bell pepper, scallion, hot sauce, salt, black pepper, and chili powder, and whisk to combine.
4. Transfer the mixture to the prepared pan, place the pan in the air fryer basket, and bake for 18 to 20 minutes, just until the frittata is set. It is important not to overcook the frittata. It should look dry and golden on the outside and be spongy in texture.
5. Slice and serve warm.

Easy Cheesy Egg Cups

Prep time: 7 minutes | Cook time: 4 minutes | Makes 6 egg cups

- 4 eggs
- 2 cups Cheddar cheese
- ½ cup cottage cheese
- ¼ cup double cream
- 1 tablespoon bacon bits
- ½ teaspoon salt
- ½ teaspoon ground black pepper

1. In a blender, combine the eggs, Cheddar cheese, cottage cheese, cream, bacon bits, salt, and pepper, and blend on high for 20 seconds.
2. Pour the egg batter into a silicone muffin mold. Place inside the air fryer basket, bake for 4 minutes, until the muffins are no longer moist on top, and serve.

Breakfast Cherry & Almond Bars
Prep time: 7 minutes | Cook time: 17 minutes | Serves 8

- 180g rolled oats
- 90g quinoa, cooked
- 90g chia seeds
- 120g prunes, pureed
- ¼ teaspoon salt
- 2 teaspoons liquid Stevia
- 180g almond butter
- 75g dried cherries, chopped
- 75g almonds, sliced

1. Preheat your air fryer to 190°C (375°F).
2. In a large mixing bowl, add quinoa, chia seeds, oats, cherries, and almonds.
3. In a saucepan over medium heat, melt almond butter, liquid Stevia and coconut oil for 2-minutes and stir to combine.
4. Add salt and prunes and mix well.
5. Pour into a baking dish that will fit inside of your air fryer and bake for 15-minutes.
6. Allow to cool for an hour once cook time is completed, then slice the bars and serve.

Salmon & Carrot Mix Breakfast
Prep time: 5 minutes | Cook time: 10 minutes | Serves 4

- 450g salmon, chopped
- 200g feta cheese, crumbled
- 4 slices of bread
- 3 tablespoons pickled red onion
- 2 cucumbers, sliced
- 1 carrot, grated

1. In a mixing bowl, combine the chopped salmon and crumbled feta cheese.
2. Add in the grated carrot, pickled red onion, and sliced cucumber, and mix well.
3. Arrange the bread slices in an oven-safe dish, and pour the salmon mixture over them.
4. Preheat your air fryer to 150˚C (300˚F) and place the dish in the air fryer basket.
5. Cook for 15 minutes or until the salmon is fully cooked.
6. Serve hot.

Breakfast Cookies
Prep time: 5 minutes | Cook time: 15 minutes | Serves 6

- ½ cup coconut flour
- 1 egg
- 1 tablespoon cream
- 3 tablespoons butter
- 4-ounces back bacon, chopped and cooked
- 1 teaspoon apple cider vinegar
- 1 teaspoon baking powder
- 1/3 teaspoon salt
- ½ cup almond flour

1. In a mixing bowl, beat the egg and whisk it.
2. Add the baking powder, cream, and apple cider vinegar to the bowl and mix.
3. Add the butter and stir gently.
4. Mix in the almond flour, coconut flour, and salt.
5. Sprinkle the mixture with the chopped cooked bacon and knead the dough.
6. Preheat the air fryer to 360°F (180°C).
7. Cover the air fryer tray with foil.
8. Form 6 medium-sized biscuits and place them in the air fryer basket.
9. Cook the biscuits for 15 minutes.
10. Once the biscuits are cooked, allow them to cool for a few minutes.
11. Transfer them onto a serving plate and serve.

Chocolate & Courgette Muffins
Prep time: 5 minutes | Cook time:36 minutes |Serves 1

- 1 tbsp ground flaxseed
- 3 tbsp water
- 120g plain flour
- 30g wholemeal flour
- 25g unsweetened cocoa powder
- ¼ tsp baking soda
- ¼ tsp sea salt
- ¼ tsp ground cinnamon
- 100g granulated sugar
- 60ml rapeseed oil
- ½ tsp vanilla extract
- ½ tsp freshly squeezed lemon juice
- 180g grated courgette
- 85g vegan chocolate chips

1. Set the air fryer temperature to 130°C. Grease 12 silicone muffin cups with non-stick cooking spray. Set aside.
2. In a small bowl, combine the ground flaxseed and water.
3. In a large mixing bowl, whisk together the plain flour, wholemeal flour, cocoa powder, baking soda, sea salt, and cinnamon. Add the granulated sugar, rapeseed oil, vanilla extract, lemon juice, and flaxseed mixture. Mix well. Fold in the grated courgette and chocolate chips.
4. Place the muffin batter into the prepared muffin cups.
5. Working in batches, place 6 muffin cups in the fryer basket and bake for 15-18 minutes or until a toothpick comes out clean from the center of a muffin.
6. Remove the muffin cups from the fryer basket and allow the muffins to cool for 10 minutes before serving.

English Breakfast
Prep time: 10 minutes | Cooking time: 20 minutes | Serves 4

- 8 medium sausages
- 8 slices of back bacon
- 4 eggs
- 8 slices of toast
- 1 can baked beans
- 2 tomatoes, sliced, sautè
- ½ cup mushrooms, finely sliced, sautè
- 1 tablespoon olive oil

1. Preheat your air fryer to 160°C (320°F).
2. Heat olive oil in a saucepan over medium-high heat.
3. Add mushrooms to the pan and sauté for a few minutes. Remove mushrooms from the pan and set aside, add tomatoes to the pan and sauté for a few minutes then set aside.
4. Place your sausages and bacon into your air fryer and cook for 10 minutes.
5. Place the baked beans into a ramekin and your (cracked) eggs in another ramekin and cook for an additional 10 minutes at 200°C (390°F).
6. Serve warm with toast on the side.

Two-Ingredient Cream Biscuits
Prep time: 10 minutes | Cook time:21 minutes |Serves 2

- 1 cup (125 g) self-rising flour
- 1/2 cup (120 ml) plus 1 tablespoon (15 ml) heavy cream
- Vegetable oil for spraying
- 2 tablespoons (28 g) unsalted butter, melted (optional)

1. Place the flour in a medium bowl and whisk to remove any lumps. Make a well in the center of the flour. While stirring with a fork, slowly pour in the cream in a steady stream. Continue to stir until the dough has mostly come together. with your hands, gather the dough, incorporating any dry flour, and form it into a ball.
2. Place the dough on a lightly floured board and pat into a rectangle that is 1/2 to 3/4 inch (1.3 to 2 cm) thick. Fold in half. Turn and repeat. One more time, pat the dough into a 3/4-inch-thick (2 cm) rectangle. Using a 2-inch (5 cm) biscuit cutter, cut out biscuits—close together to minimize waste—taking care not to twist the cutter when pulling it up. You should be able to cut out 5 biscuits. Gather up any scraps and cut out 1 or 2 more biscuits. (These may be misshapen and slightly tougher than the first 5 biscuits, but still delicious.)
3. Preheat the air fryer to 325°F (170°C) for 3 minutes. Spray the air fryer basket with oil to prevent sticking. Place the biscuits in the air fryer basket so that they are barely touching. Cook for 15 to 18 minutes until the tops are browned and the insides fully cooked. Remove the biscuits to a plate, brush the tops with melted butter, if using, and serve.

Granola-Stuffed Baked Apples
Prep time: 5 minutes | Cook time:20 minutes |Serves 2

- 4 Granny Smith or other firm apples
- 1 cup (100 g) granola
- 2 tablespoons (19 g) light brown sugar
- 3/4 teaspoon cinnamon
- 2 tablespoons (28 g) unsalted butter, melted
- 1 cup (240 ml) water or apple juice

1. Working one apple at a time, cut a circle around the apple stem and scoop out the core, taking care not to cut all the way through to the bottom. (This should leave an empty cavity in the middle of the apple for the granola.) Repeat with the remaining apples.
2. In a small bowl, combine the granola, brown sugar, and cinnamon. Pour the melted butter over the ingredients and stir with a fork. Divide the granola mixture among the apples, packing it tightly into the empty cavity.
3. Place the apples in the cake pan insert for the air fryer. Pour the water or juice around the apples. Bake at 350°F (180°C) for 20 minutes until the apples are soft all the way through. (If the granola begins to scorch before the apples are fully

cooked, cover the top of the apples with a small piece of aluminum foil.)
4. Serve warm with a dollop of crème fraîche or yogurt, if desired.

Black Bean Burger Burritos
Prep time: 20 minutes | Cook time:10 minutes |Serves 1

- 4 black bean burgers
- Sriracha chili sauce
- 4 large flour tortillas
- Baby spinach
- 1 avocado, diced

1. Preheat the air fryer to 380°F (190°C).
2. Place the black bean burgers in the fryer basket and cook for 4 minutes per side.
3. Remove the burgers from the fryer basket and roughly chop. Spread the chili sauce on the tortillas and top with equal amounts of spinach, avocado, and burger. Wrap the tortillas around the filling.
4. Place the burritos in the fryer basket and cook until the tortillas are toasted, about 2 minutes.
5. Remove the burritos from the fryer basket and cut in half. Serve immediately or wrap them in aluminum foil for an on-the-go meal.

Bacon & Cheddar Scrambled Eggs
Prep time: 5 minutes | Cook time: 10 minutes | Serves 4

- ¼ teaspoon onion powder
- 4 eggs, beaten
- 3-ounces bacon, cooked, chopped
- 120g cheddar cheese, grated
- 3 tablespoons Greek yoghurt
- ¼ teaspoon garlic powder
- Salt and pepper to taste

1. Preheat your air fryer to 165°C (330°F).
2. Whisk eggs in a bowl, add salt and pepper to taste along with yoghurt, garlic powder, onion powder, cheese, and bacon, stir.
3. Add the egg mixture into an oven-proof baking dish.
4. Place into air fryer and cook for 10-minutes.
5. Scramble eggs and serve warm.

Baked Eggs & Sausage Muffins
Prep time: 10 minutes | Cooking time: 20 minutes | Serves 2

- 3 eggs
- 60ml double cream
- 2 sausages, boiled
- Chopped fresh herbs
- Sea salt to taste
- 4 tablespoons cheese, grated
- 1 piece of bread, sliced lengthwise

1. Preheat your air fryer to 180°C.
2. Break the eggs in a bowl, add cream, and scramble.
3. Grease 3 muffin cups with cooking spray. Add equal amounts of egg mixture into each. Arrange sliced sausages and bread slices into muffin cups, sinking into egg mixture. Sprinkle the tops with cheese, and salt to taste.
4. Cook the muffins for 20 minutes.
5. Season with fresh herbs and serve warm.

Spinach & Parsley Baked Omelet
Prep time: 10 minutes | Cooking time: 10 minutes | Serves 1

- 1 teaspoon olive oil
- 3 eggs
- 3 tablespoons ricotta cheese
- 1 tablespoon parsley, chopped
- ¼ cup spinach, chopped
- Salt and pepper to taste

1. Preheat your air fryer to 165˚C.
2. Whisk eggs adding salt and pepper as seasoning.
3. Heat the olive oil in air fryer. Stir in the ricotta, spinach, and parsley with eggs. Pour the egg mixture into baking dish and cook in air fryer for 10-minutes.
4. Serve warm.

Italian Egg Cups
Prep time: 5 minutes | Cook time:10 minutes |Serves 4

- Olive oil
- 250g tomato passata
- 4 medium free-range eggs
- 4 tablespoons shredded mozzarella cheese
- 4 teaspoons grated Parmesan cheese
- Salt
- Freshly ground black pepper
- Chopped fresh basil, for garnish

1. Lightly grease 4 individual ramekins with olive oil.
2. Divide ¼ cup of tomato passata between each ramekin.
3. Crack one egg into each ramekin on top of the tomato passata.
4. Sprinkle 1 tablespoon of mozzarella and 1 tablespoon of Parmesan on top of each egg. Season with salt and pepper.
5. Cover each ramekin with aluminium foil. Place two of the ramekins in the air fryer basket.
6. Air fry for 5 minutes and remove the aluminium foil. Air fry until the top is lightly browned and the egg white is cooked, another 2 to 4 minutes. If you prefer the yolk to be firmer, cook for 3 to 5 more minutes.
7. Repeat with the remaining two ramekins. Garnish with basil and serve.

Chapter 4
Snack Recipes

Egg Roll Pizza Sticks

Prep time: 10 minutes | Cook time:5 minutes |Serves 4

- Olive oil
- 8 pieces reduced-fat mozzarella cheese string cheese
- 8 spring roll wrappers
- 24 slices turkey pepperoni
- Tomato passata, for dipping (optional)

1. Preheat the air fryer to 180°C (350°F). Lightly brush the fryer basket with olive oil.
2. Lay each spring roll wrapper diagonally on a work surface, so it looks like a diamond.
3. Place 3 slices of turkey pepperoni in a vertical line down the center of the wrapper.
4. Place 1 piece of mozzarella string cheese on top of the turkey pepperoni.
5. Fold the top and bottom corners of the spring roll wrapper over the cheese stick.
6. Fold the left corner over the cheese stick and roll the cheese stick up to resemble a spring roll. Dip a finger in water and seal the edge of the roll.
7. Repeat with the rest of the pizza sticks.
8. Place them in the fryer basket in a single layer, making sure to leave a little space between each one. Lightly brush the pizza sticks with oil. You may need to cook these in batches.
9. Air fry until the pizza sticks are lightly browned and crispy, about 5 minutes.
10. These are best served hot while the cheese is melted. Accompany with a small bowl of tomato passata, if desired. Enjoy!

Lemon Bars

Prep time: 25 minutes | Cook time:22 minutes |Serves 1

- 4 tbsp coconut oil, melted
- ¼ tsp plus 1 pinch of sea salt
- 1 tsp pure vanilla extract
- ½ cup plus 3 tbsp caster sugar
- ½ cup plus 2 tbsp plain flour
- ¼ cup freshly squeezed lemon juice
- zest of 1 lemon
- ½ cup canned coconut cream
- 4 tbsp cornflour
- icing sugar

1. Set the air fryer temp to 350°F (180°C).
2. In a medium bowl, combine the coconut oil, ¼ teaspoon of salt, vanilla extract, and 3 tablespoons of sugar. Mix in the flour until a soft dough forms. Transfer the mixture to a baking dish and gently press the dough to cover the bottom.
3. Place the dish in the fryer basket and bake until golden, about 10 minutes. Remove the crust from the fryer basket and set aside to cool slightly.
4. In a medium saucepan on the stove over medium heat, combine the lemon juice and zest, coconut cream, the pinch of sea salt, and the remaining ½ cup of sugar,. Whisk in the cornflour and cook

until thickened, about 5 minutes. Pour the lemon mixture over the crust.

5. Place the dish in the fryer basket and cook until the mixture is bubbly and almost completely set, about 10 to 12 minutes.
6. Remove the dish from the fryer basket and set aside to cool completely. Transfer the dish to the refrigerator for at least 4 hours. Dust with the icing sugar and slice into 6 bars before serving.

Peanut Butter Cookies

Prep time: 10 minutes | Cook time:10 minutes |Serves 1

- 1 tbsp ground flaxseed
- 3 tbsp water
- 240g creamy peanut butter (Skippy recommended)
- 150g light brown sugar
- 90g all-purpose flour
- 1 tsp baking soda
- ½ tsp salt

1. In a small bowl, combine the flaxseed and water. Mix well and set aside for 5 minutes.
2. In a large bowl, combine the peanut butter and brown sugar. Add the flaxseed mixture, flour, baking soda, and salt. Mix until a soft dough forms. Refrigerate the dough for at least 20 minutes.
3. Preheat the air fryer to 165°C (330°F).
4. Spray the fryer basket with nonstick cooking spray.
5. Use a small scoop or tablespoon to roll the dough into 18 equally sized balls. Use a fork to press a diagonal hash mark into each ball.
6. Working in batches, place 9 balls in the fryer basket and cook until slightly golden, about 5 minutes.
7. Transfer the cookies to a wire rack to cool before serving.

Roasted Garlic Guacamole with Homemade Tortilla Chips

Prep time: 5 minutes | Cook time: 53 minutes |Serves 4

- 1 bulb of garlic
- 1 teaspoon vegetable oil
- 1 green chili pepper
- 4 ripe avocados
- 3 tablespoons (45 ml) freshly squeezed lime juice
- 1 teaspoon ground cumin
- 1 teaspoon sea salt
- Pinch of cayenne pepper
- 1/2 red onion, finely chopped
- 2 plum tomatoes, deseeded and finely chopped
- 12 corn tortillas
- Vegetable oil for brushing
- 3 teaspoons sea salt

1. Preheat the oven to 180°C (fan)/200°C/gas mark 6. Cut the top off the garlic bulb to expose the cloves. Drizzle with oil and wrap in foil. Roast in the oven for 30-40 minutes until soft. Remove from the oven, unwrap and let cool. Squeeze out the garlic cloves into a large bowl.
2. Cut the green chili pepper in half lengthways and remove the seeds. Place the pepper in the air fryer basket and cook at 200°C for 10-12 minutes until charred. Once cool enough to handle, remove the skin and finely chop the flesh. Add to the bowl with the roasted garlic.
3. Halve the avocados and remove the pits. Scoop out the flesh into the bowl with the garlic and chili. Mash everything together. Add the lime juice, ground cumin, 1 teaspoon of sea salt, and cayenne pepper, and mix well. Stir in the chopped red onion and tomato. Taste and adjust the seasoning if needed. Cover the guacamole with plastic wrap and chill until needed.
4. To make the tortilla chips, brush the corn tortillas with oil and sprinkle each one with 1/4 teaspoon of sea salt. Cut each tortilla into 6 wedges. Preheat the air fryer to 200°C. Working in batches, spread the tortilla wedges in a single layer in the air fryer basket. Cook for 4 to 6 minutes, turning once halfway through, until crisp. Remove and repeat with the remaining chips. Allow the chips to cool before serving.

Easy Mac and Cheese Bites

Prep time: 10 minutes, plus at least 3 hours to chill | Cook time: 16 to 20 minutes | Makes 8 balls

- 3 cups prepared macaroni and cheese, homemade or store-bought
- 2 eggs
- 1½ cups breadcrumbs
- 1 tablespoon chopped fresh chives

1. Line the air fryer basket with parchment paper.
2. Chill the prepared macaroni and cheese in the refrigerator until firm, at least 3 hours.
3. Scoop and roll the cold macaroni and cheese into 1½- to 2-inch balls, making about 8 total.
4. In a small bowl, beat the eggs.
5. Put the breadcrumbs in another small bowl.
6. Working one at a time, dip the macaroni and cheese balls in the egg, then roll them in the breadcrumbs.
7. Place in the lined air fryer basket and fry for 8 to 10 minutes per batch, until golden and crispy.
8. Sprinkle with the chives when serving.

Tandoori Yogurt Dip with Naan Breadsticks

Prep time: 5 minutes | Cook time: 6 minutes |Serves 4

- 2 cups (460 g) plain Greek yogurt, preferably full fat
- 1 clove garlic, minced
- 1 tablespoon (6 g) Tandoori Spice Mix (see below), divided
- Juice and zest of $1/2$ lemon
- 1 tablespoon (15 ml) extra-virgin olive oil plus extra for brushing
- 3 large naan
- 1 teaspoon cumin
- 1 teaspoon coriander
- 1 teaspoon ginger
- 1 teaspoon kosher salt
- $1/2$ teaspoon paprika
- $1/2$ teaspoon cayenne pepper
- $1/2$ teaspoon turmeric

1. To make the tandoori spice mix, whisk together the spices in a small bowl until well combined.
2. In a large bowl, combine the yogurt, garlic, 1 tablespoon (6 g) of the tandoori spice mix, lemon juice and zest, and olive oil. Stir until thoroughly mixed. Refrigerate for 1 hour to allow the flavors to develop.
3. To make the naan chips, brush the naan with olive oil and sprinkle each piece with some of the tandoori spice mix to taste. Slice the bread into $1^1/2$-inch (4 cm) strips and cut the longer strips in half. Working in batches, arrange the naan chips in a single layer in the basket of the air fryer. Cook at 360°F (182°C) for 4 to 6 minutes, turning once halfway through, until browned on both sides and crispy. Serve the naan chips warm with the yogurt dip.

Spiced Nuts

Prep time: 5 minutes | Cook time: 10 minutes | Serves 3 cups

- 1 cup almonds
- 1 cup pecan halves
- 1 cup cashews
- 1 egg white, beaten
- ½ teaspoon ground cinnamon
- Pinch of cayenne pepper
- ¼ teaspoon ground cloves
- Dash of salt

1. In a mixing bowl, whisk together the egg white with the spices.
2. Preheat your air fryer to 150°C/300°F.
3. Add the nuts to the spiced mixture and toss to coat evenly.
4. Place the spiced nuts in the air fryer basket in a single layer.
5. Air fry for 10 minutes, shaking the basket every 3-4 minutes to ensure even cooking.
6. Once the nuts are lightly browned and toasted, remove them from the air fryer and let them cool before serving.

Zucchini Fondue with Lobsters

Prep time: 10 minutes | Cooking time: 1 hour 5 minutes | Serves 4

- 1 kg cooked lobster
- 800 g courgettes (zucchini)
- 2 large onions
- 6 sprigs of fresh mint
- 1 tbsp. olive oil
- 1/2 lemon, juiced
- Salt and pepper, to taste
- Coarse sea salt, to serve

1. Wash the courgettes, dry, trim the ends, and cut into 5mm slices.
2. Peel and chop the onions. Heat the olive oil in a frying pan and sauté the onion.
3. Add the courgettes, salt, and pepper. Cook in the air fryer for 40 minutes, stirring occasionally to prevent sticking to the bottom. When the mixture becomes tender, add the lemon juice and minced mint.
4. Arrange the zucchini fondue and lobster meat on a serving platter. Serve with coarse sea salt on the side.

Savory Dough Nuggets

Prep time: 15 minutes| Cook time: 3 to 8 minutes|Makes 20 nuggets

- 120g plain flour, plus more for dusting
- 1/4 teaspoon salt
- 1 teaspoon baking powder
- 1/2 teaspoon butter, at room temperature, plus more for brushing
- 60 to 120ml water
- Olive oil spray
- 1/4 teaspoon garlic powder
- 1/8 teaspoon onion powder
- 1/8 teaspoon seasoned salt

1. Place a parchment liner in the air fryer basket.
2. In a large bowl, combine the flour, salt, baking powder, and 1/2 teaspoon of butter. Cut the ingredients together using a fork or pastry cutter.
3. Add the water and mix well. The mixture should be soft and not sticky. If it is too sticky, work in more flour.
4. Roll out the dough on a lightly floured surface until it is about 1.25 cm thick.
5. Cut into vertical strips and then cross over with horizontal strips, giving you 2.5- to 5-cm squares.
6. Place the dough on the liner in the fryer basket in a single layer.
7. Spray with olive oil.
8. In a small bowl, combine the garlic powder, onion powder, and seasoned salt, then sprinkle the mixture on top of the dough.
9. Fry for 3 to 4 minutes, until golden. Immediately brush with butter once the nuggets are done cooking. Repeat with any remaining dough and serve.

Greek-Style Mushrooms

Prep time: 10 minutes | Cooking time: 20 minutes | Serves 2

- 5 tsp. lemon juice
- 2 bay leaves
- 1 tsp. coriander seeds
- 1 tsp. black pepper
- 700 g mushrooms
- 4 tsp. minced parsley
- Salt, to taste

1. Place a liter of water in a saucepan and add lemon juice, bay leaves, coriander seeds, and black pepper. Season with salt.
2. Bring the water to a boil and cook the mushrooms in the air fryer for 10 minutes.
3. Remove the stems from the mushrooms, wash quickly, drain, and cut into pieces.
4. Set the timer for 2 minutes and turn off the heat.
5. Add the parsley and gently mix. Let it cool completely in the broth.
6. Drain the mushrooms, place them on a plate, and drizzle with the cooking broth, adding some coriander seeds.

Keto Chips

Prep time: 5 minutes | Cook time: 20 minutes | Serves 4

- 1 large rutabaga, peeled, cut into spears about ¼ inch wide
- Salt and pepper to taste
- ½ teaspoon paprika
- 2 tablespoons coconut oil

1. Preheat your air fryer to 232°C.
2. Mix the oil, paprika, salt, and pepper.
3. Pour the oil mixture over the fries, making sure all pieces are well coated.
4. Cook in air fryer for 20-minutes or until crispy.

Sweet and Smoky Candied Pecans

Prep time: 5 minutes | Cook time: 12 minutes | Serves 2

- 1 pound (455 g) pecan halves
- 2 egg whites
- 1/2 cup (115 g) brown sugar
- 1 tablespoon (7 g) cumin
- 2 teaspoons smoked paprika
- 2 teaspoons kosher salt

1. Toss the pecans with the egg whites in a medium bowl. Add the sugar and spices and toss to coat the pecans with the seasoning.
2. Place half the pecans in the basket of the air fryer. Cook at 150°C (300°F) for 10 to 12 minutes, checking frequently and shaking the basket, until the nuts taste toasty and caramelized but not burnt.
3. Remove the basket from the air fryer and spread the pecans on a baking sheet to cool. They will firm up and become crispy as they cool.
4. Repeat with the remaining pecans.
5. Store in an airtight container until needed. They will last up to 2 weeks.

Cheese & Onion Nuggets

Prep time: 5 minutes | Cook time: 12 minutes | Serves 4

- 200g Edam cheese, grated
- 2 spring onions, finely chopped
- 1 egg, beaten
- 1 tablespoon vegetable oil
- 1 tablespoon thyme, dried
- Salt and pepper to taste

1. In a mixing bowl, combine the grated cheese, chopped spring onions, vegetable oil, thyme, salt and pepper.
2. Form the mixture into 8 small balls and press down the center to create a well.
3. Chill the nuggets in the fridge for about an hour.
4. Using a pastry brush, carefully brush the beaten egg over the nuggets.
5. Preheat the air fryer to 180°C (350°F).
6. Place the nuggets in the air fryer basket and cook for 12 minutes, or until golden brown and crispy.

Party Pigs In Blankets

Prep time: 8 minutes | Cook time: 16 minutes | Makes 16 rolls

- 1 small package cocktail sausages
- 1 sheet ready-rolled puff pastry
- 2 tablespoons butter, melted
- 1 teaspoon onion powder
- 2 teaspoons sesame seeds

1. Preheat the air fryer to 180°C (356°F).
2. Remove the cocktail sausages from the package and dry them completely with a paper towel.
3. Unroll the puff pastry sheet and cut it into 16 equal strips.
4. Place each sausage at the end of a pastry strip and roll it up.
5. Place the "pigs in blankets" on a plate and brush them with melted butter.
6. Sprinkle with onion powder and sesame seeds.
7. Working in batches, place half of the "pigs" in the air fryer basket and bake for about 8 minutes or until golden brown.
8. Repeat with any remaining pieces and serve.

Mexican Potato Skins
Prep time: 10 minutes | Cook time:55 minutes |Serves 6

- Olive oil
- 6 medium baking potatoes, scrubbed
- Salt
- Freshly ground black pepper
- 240g fat-free refried black beans
- 1 tablespoon taco seasoning
- 120ml salsa
- 75g reduced-fat grated Cheddar cheese
- Instructions:

1. Preheat your air fryer to 200°C (180°C fan)/400°F/ Gas Mark 6.
2. Brush the potatoes with olive oil and season with salt and pepper. Prick each potato with a fork.
3. Place the potatoes in the air fryer basket and cook until fork-tender, for about 40-50 minutes.
4. In a small bowl, mix the refried black beans and taco seasoning.
5. Once the potatoes are cool enough to handle, cut each one in half lengthways and scoop out most of the insides, leaving about ¼ inch in the skins so the potato skins hold their shape.
6. Season the insides of the potato skins with salt and black pepper. Brush the insides with olive oil.
7. Put the potato skins back into the air fryer basket, skin side down, and cook for 8-10 minutes or until crisp and golden.
8. Place the potato skins on a work surface, spoon ½ tablespoon of seasoned refried black beans into each one, and top each with 2 teaspoons of salsa and 1 tablespoon of grated Cheddar cheese.
9. Return the filled potato skins to the air fryer basket in a single layer and brush lightly with olive oil.
10. Cook for 2-3 minutes or until the cheese is melted and bubbly.
11. Serve hot with extra salsa, if desired. Enjoy your Mexican potato skins!

Grilled Pineapple with Cinnamon
Prep time: 5 minutes | Cook time: 20 minutes | Serves 2

- 4 slices of fresh pineapple
- 2 tablespoons of brown sugar
- 1 teaspoon of ground cinnamon

1. In a small bowl, mix together the brown sugar and cinnamon.
2. Add the pineapple slices to the bowl and toss until they are evenly coated with the sugar mixture.
3. Leave to marinate in the fridge for 20 minutes.
4. Preheat your air fryer to 180°C (350°F) for 5 minutes.
5. Place the pineapple slices in the air fryer basket, making sure they are in a single layer and not touching each other.
6. Air fry for 10 minutes.
7. Flip the pineapple slices over and air fry for an additional 5-10 minutes or until they are golden brown and caramelized on both sides.
8. Serve immediately, garnished with fresh mint leaves if desired.
9. Enjoy your delicious Grilled Pineapple with Cinnamon!

Garlic & Ginger Sugar Snow Peas
Prep time: 5 minutes | Cook time: 8 minutes | Serves 4

- 500g sugar snap peas, trimmed
- 1 teaspoon olive oil
- 1 teaspoon black pepper
- 1 teaspoon sea salt
- 1 tablespoon rice vinegar
- 1 tablespoon soy sauce
- 2 cloves garlic, minced
- 3cm piece of ginger, minced

1. Wash the sugar snap peas with cold running water and trim the ends.
2. Clean the ginger and garlic with water, then slice them into small pieces.
3. In a large bowl, add a tablespoon of soy sauce, a tablespoon of rice vinegar, salt, pepper, and olive oil.
4. Mix in the minced ginger and garlic.
5. Add trimmed sugar snap peas and toss to combine.
6. Soak the peas in the marinade for about an hour before air frying them.
7. Preheat your air fryer to 190°C (375°F) for 2 minutes.
8. Transfer the marinated peas into the air fryer and cook for 4 minutes.
9. Toss sugar snap peas and cook for an additional 4 minutes.

Chapter 5
Poultry Recipes

Cajun Chicken Kebabs

Prep time: 20 minutes | Cook time:20 minutes |Serves 6

- Olive oil
- 680g boneless, skinless chicken breasts, cut into bite-sized chunks
- 1½ tablespoons Cajun seasoning, divided
- 1 medium red bell pepper, cut into big chunks
- 1 medium green bell pepper, cut into big chunks
- 1 medium onion, cut into big chunks

1. Lightly brush an air fryer basket with olive oil.
2. In a large bowl, toss the chicken with 1 tablespoon of Cajun seasoning, and brush with olive oil to coat.
3. In a separate, large bowl, toss the bell peppers and onion with the remaining ½ tablespoon of Cajun seasoning, and brush with olive oil to coat.
4. If using wooden skewers, soak them in water for at least 30 minutes before using.
5. Thread the chicken and vegetables onto the skewers, alternating with chicken, then vegetable.
6. Place the skewers in the air fryer basket in a single layer. You may need to cook them in batches.
7. Air fry at 180°C for 10 minutes. Flip the skewers over and lightly brush with olive oil. Air fry until the chicken has an internal temperature of at least 74°C, another 5 to 10 minutes.

Israeli Chicken Schnitzel

Prep time: 5 minutes | Cook time: 8 minutes |Serves 4

- 2 large boneless, skinless chicken breasts, each weighing about 1 pound (455 g)
- 1 cup (125 g) all-purpose flour
- 2 teaspoons garlic powder
- 2 teaspoons kosher salt
- 1 teaspoon black pepper
- 1 teaspoon paprika
- 2 eggs beaten with 2 tablespoons (30 ml) water
- 2 cups (100 g) panko bread crumbs
- Vegetable oil for spraying
- Lemon for serving

1. Place 1 of the chicken breasts between 2 pieces of plastic wrap. Use a mallet or a rolling pin to pound the chicken until it is $1/4$ inch (6 mm) thick. Set aside. Repeat with the second breast. Whisk together the flour, garlic powder, salt, pepper, and paprika on a large plate. Place the panko in a separate shallow bowl or pie plate.
2. Dredge 1 of the chicken breasts in the flour, shaking off any excess, then dip it in the egg mixture. Dredge the chicken breast in the panko, making sure to coat it completely. Shake off any excess panko. Place the battered chicken breast on a plate. Repeat with the second chicken breast.
3. Spray the basket of the air fryer with oil. Place 1 of the battered chicken breasts in the basket and spray the top with oil. Cook at 375°F (190°C) until the top is browned, about 5 minutes. Flip the chicken and spray the second side with oil. Cook until the second side is browned and crispy and the internal temperature reaches 165°F (71°C). Remove the first chicken breast from the air fryer and repeat the process with the second chicken breast. Serve hot with plenty of lemons for squeezing.

Easy General Tso's Chicken

Prep time: 10 minutes | Cook time: 21 minutes| Makes 3 cups

FOR THE SAUCE

- 3 teaspoons sesame oil
- 1 teaspoon minced garlic
- ½ teaspoon ground ginger
- ½ cup chicken stock
- 1 tablespoon soy sauce
- ½ teaspoon hot sauce, plus more for serving
- 1 tablespoon hoisin sauce
- 1 tablespoon cornflour

FOR THE CHICKEN

- 2 boneless, skinless chicken breasts, cut into 1-inch pieces
- 1 tablespoon soy sauce
- 1 tablespoon cornflour
- Cooking spray
- 1 medium spring onion, finely chopped, for garnish
- Sesame seeds, for garnish

TO MAKE THE SAUCE

1. In a small saucepan over low heat, combine the sesame oil, garlic, and ginger, and cook for 1 minute.
2. Add the stock, soy sauce, hot sauce, and hoisin, and whisk to combine.
3. Whisk in the cornflour and continue cooking over low heat until the sauce starts to thicken, about 5 minutes. Remove from the heat, cover, and set aside.

TO MAKE THE CHICKEN

4. In a medium bowl, put the chicken, soy sauce, and cornflour. Toss to combine.
5. Place the chicken in the air fryer basket, spray with cooking spray, and bake for 16 minutes, stopping halfway through to toss the chicken and spray with a little more cooking spray. Continue cooking until the internal temperature reaches 82°C and the juices run clear.
6. Once the chicken is done cooking, transfer to a large bowl and toss with the prepared sauce.
7. Top with the spring onion and sesame seeds, and serve.

Tandoori-Style Chicken Skewers

Prep time: 5 minutes | Cook time: 30 minutes |Serves 4

- 11/2 pounds (680 g) hand-filleted boneless, skinless chicken breast or regular boneless, skinless chicken breast pounded to 1/4-inch (6 mm) thickness
- 4 cloves garlic, peeled
- 1 piece (1 inch [2.5 cm]) fresh ginger, peeled
- 1 cup (230 g) plain yogurt, preferably full fat
- 1 tablespoon (6 g) Tandoori Spice Mix
- 1 teaspoon kosher salt
- Juice and zest of 1 lime plus more for serving
- Vegetable oil for spraying

1. Cut the chicken breast into strips approximately 1 inch (2.5 cm) wide and place in a glass baking dish. Mince the garlic and ginger together very finely to form a chunky paste. Whisk the garlic-ginger paste with the yogurt, spice mix, salt, and lime zest and juice in a medium bowl until combined. Pour the yogurt mixture into the baking dish with the chicken and turn the chicken pieces until they are coated. Cover the dish and refrigerate at least 20 minutes and up to 6 hours.
2. Preheat the air fryer to 400°F (200°C). If desired, thread half the chicken pieces onto metal skewers designed for the air fryer and place them on a rack. Alternatively, you can simply spray the air fryer basket with oil to prevent sticking and lay half the chicken pieces in the basket. Cook at 400°F (200°C) for 10 minutes, turning once halfway through. Repeat with the remaining chicken pieces.
3. Serve immediately with additional lime wedges for spritzing.

Turkey and Rosemary Butter

Prep time: 5 minutes | Cooking time: 24 minutes | Serves 4

- 1 turkey breast
- A pinch of salt and black pepper
- Juice of 1 lemon
- 2 tablespoons rosemary, chopped
- 2 tablespoons butter, melted

1. In a bowl, mix the butter with the rosemary, lemon juice, salt, and pepper and whisk really well.
2. Brush the turkey pieces with the rosemary butter and place them in the air fryer basket. Cook at 190°C for 12 minutes on each side.
3. Divide between plates and serve with a side salad.

Turkey and Shallot Sauce

Prep time: 5 minutes | Cooking time: 30 minutes | Serves 4

- 1 large turkey breast
- 1 tablespoon olive oil
- ¼ teaspoon sweet paprika
- Salt and black pepper, to taste
- 1 cup chicken stock
- 3 tablespoons butter, melted
- 4 shallots, chopped

1. Preheat the air fryer to 180°C (350°F).
2. Heat up a frying pan with the olive oil and butter over medium-high heat. Add the turkey chunks and brown for 3 minutes on each side.
3. Add the chopped shallots, stir and sauté for 5 minutes more.
4. Add the paprika, chicken stock, salt and pepper. Stir well.
5. Transfer the mixture to an oven-safe dish and place it in the air fryer.
6. Air fry for 20 minutes or until the turkey is cooked through.
7. Divide into bowls and serve hot.

Sweet and Sour Chicken

Prep time: 10 minutes | Cook time: 30 minutes | Makes 4 cups

FOR THE SAUCE:
- 1 teaspoon minced garlic
- 227g canned pineapple chunks, juice reserved
- ½ green bell pepper, chopped
- 20g diced red onion
- 410ml water
- 150g granulated sugar
- 120ml malt vinegar
- 1 tablespoon soy sauce or gluten-free tamari
- 30g cornflour

FOR THE CHICKEN:
- 2 boneless, skinless chicken breasts
- 60g cornflour
- Rapeseed oil spray

1. In a small saucepan over low heat, combine the garlic, pineapple chunks and juice, bell pepper, red onion, water, sugar, vinegar, and soy sauce. Bring to a simmer.
2. Whisk in the cornflour and continue cooking for about 5 minutes, until the sauce has thickened. Remove from the heat, cover, and set aside.
3. Meanwhile, cut the chicken into 1-inch pieces.
4. In a large bowl, toss the chicken with the cornflour to coat.
5. Put the chicken in the air fryer basket, spray with rapeseed oil, and fry for 25 minutes, stopping halfway through to remove the fryer basket, toss the chicken, and spray with more rapeseed oil. Continue cooking until the internal temperature has reached 82°C and the juices run clear.
6. Remove the chicken from the air fryer, and transfer it to a large bowl.
7. Pour the sauce over the cooked chicken, toss to coat, and serve.

Garlic Chicken Nuggets

Prep time: 10minutes | Cook time: 10 minutes | Serves 4

- 75g breadcrumbs
- 250g chicken breast, thinly chopped
- 1 teaspoon parsley
- 2 eggs, divided
- 1 teaspoon tomato ketchup
- 1 tablespoon olive oil
- Salt and pepper to taste
- 1 teaspoon garlic, minced
- 1 teaspoon paprika

1. Mix breadcrumbs, salt, pepper, paprika, and oil.
2. Mix well to make a thick paste.
3. Mix chopped chicken, ketchup, one egg, parsley in a bowl.
4. Shape the chicken mixture into little nugget shapes and dip into other beaten egg.
5. Coat the nuggets with breadcrumbs.
6. Cook at 200˚C for 10 minutes in air fryer.

Spinach and Feta Chicken Meatballs

Prep time: 30 minutes | Cook time:18 minutes |Serves 6

- Olive oil
- 113 grams fresh spinach, chopped
- ½ teaspoon salt, plus more as needed
- 60 grams wholemeal breadcrumbs
- ¼ teaspoon freshly ground black pepper
- ¼ teaspoon garlic powder
- 1 egg, beaten
- 454 grams lean minced chicken
- 75 grams crumbled feta cheese

1. Grease a large frying pan lightly with olive oil. Add the spinach, season lightly with salt, and cook over medium heat until the spinach has wilted, 2 to 3 minutes. Set aside.
2. In a large bowl, mix together the breadcrumbs, ½ teaspoon of salt, pepper, and garlic powder. Add the egg, chicken, spinach, and feta and stir to gently combine.
3. Using a heaping tablespoon, form 24 meatballs.
4. Lightly grease a air fryer basket with olive oil.
5. Place the meatballs in the air fryer basket in a single layer. Spray the meatballs lightly with olive oil. You may need to cook them in batches.
6. Air fry for 7 minutes. Turn the meatballs over and cook until golden brown, an additional 5 to 8 minutes.

Turkey, Mushroom & Egg Casserole

Prep time: 5 minutes | Cook time: 15 minutes | Serves 4

- 6 eggs
- 225g spinach
- 125g shredded cheddar cheese
- 2 onions, chopped
- 28g cooked turkey, diced
- 4 mushrooms, diced
- Pinch of onion powder
- Salt and pepper to taste
- Pinch of garlic powder
- 1/4 green bell pepper, chopped

1. Preheat your air fryer to 200°C.
2. Whisk the eggs in mixing bowl.
3. Add mushrooms, garlic powder, bell pepper, onion powder, onions, 100g cheese, and cooked diced turkey.
4. Mix well and add mixture to casserole dish.
5. Sprinkle the top of mixture with remaining cheese.
6. Add spinach on top.
7. Bake in air fryer for 15 minutes. Serve hot!

Spinach-Stuffed Chicken Parmesan

Prep time: 10 minutes | Cook time: 13 to 14 minutes | Makes 2 chicken breasts

- 50g breadcrumbs
- 30g grated Parmesan cheese, divided
- 50g fresh baby spinach, chopped
- 50g ricotta cheese
- 1 egg
- 2 chicken breasts, cut into slices and pounded thin
- Olive oil spray
- 2 tablespoons tomato sauce
- 50g mozzarella cheese
- Salt
- Ground black pepper

1. In a medium bowl, stir to combine the breadcrumbs with about half of the Parmesan cheese. Set aside.
2. In another medium bowl, combine the spinach, ricotta, and remaining half of the Parmesan cheese. Mix together with a fork until well combined.
3. In a small, shallow bowl, whisk the egg with a fork.
4. Lay the chicken out on a baking sheet sprayed with oil or lined with parchment paper, and spread about 2 tablespoons of the spinach mixture on top of each piece.
5. Roll up each piece, securing the end with a toothpick.
6. Dip each chicken roll in the egg and then in the breadcrumb mixture to coat.
7. Place the chicken rolls seam-side down in the fryer basket. Spray with olive oil and air fry for 12 minutes, or until the internal temperature reaches 82°C and the juices run clear. (Angle the thermometer to hit the thickest part of the chicken.)
8. Remove from the air fryer, and spoon 1 tablespoon of the tomato sauce over each chicken roll.
9. Top with the mozzarella cheese and return to the air fryer. Air fry for another 1 to 2 minutes, until the cheese melts, and serve.

Fried Turkey Breast

Prep time: 5 minutes | Cook time: 30 minutes | Serves 5

- 3.2 kg turkey breast, skinless and boneless
- 2 tablespoons olive oil
- 1/2 teaspoon ground cumin
- Salt and black pepper to taste

1. Rub the whole turkey breast with all seasonings and olive oil.
2. Preheat your air fryer to 170°C and cook the turkey for 15 minutes.
3. Flip the breast over and cook for another 15 minutes.
4. Slice turkey and serve with fresh vegetables.

Teriyaki Chicken Kebabs

Prep time: 10 minutes | Cook time: 9 to 10 minutes | Makes 4 kebabs

FOR THE GLAZE
- 3 tablespoons honey
- 3 tablespoons soy sauce
- ½ teaspoon salt
- ½ teaspoon freshly ground black pepper

FOR THE SKEWERS
- 1 bell pepper, any color, chopped
- 6 small chestnut mushrooms, cut in half
- ½ cup pineapple chunks
- 4 boneless, skinless chicken thighs, cut into cubes or strips
- Olive oil spray
- ¼ teaspoon sesame seeds

1. Preheat the air fryer to 400°F (200°C).
2. In a small bowl, mix together the honey, soy sauce, salt, and pepper to make the glaze.
3. In separate small bowls, place the bell pepper, mushrooms, and pineapple chunks.
4. Thread the chicken, bell pepper, mushrooms, and pineapple onto skewers, alternating the ingredients until each skewer is full.
5. Place the skewers in the air fryer basket, and lightly spray with olive oil.
6. Air fry for 8 minutes, or until the chicken is cooked through and reaches an internal temperature of 165°F (74°C) and the juices run clear.
7. Brush the skewers with the teriyaki glaze, then air fry for another 1 to 2 minutes, or until the glaze has thickened and caramelized.
8. Sprinkle with sesame seeds before serving.

Roasted Whole Chicken with Herbs

Prep time: 5 minutes | Cook time: 40 minutes | Serves 4

- 2.27 kg whole chicken with skin
- 30 ml extra-virgin olive oil
- ½ teaspoon rosemary
- ½ teaspoon basil
- ½ teaspoon thyme
- 1 teaspoon onion powder
- 1 teaspoon garlic powder
- Salt and black pepper to taste

1. Rub the chicken with salt, herbs, pepper, and olive oil.
2. Set aside for 30-minutes.
3. Preheat your air fryer to 170°C.
4. Cook chicken for 20 minutes then turn.
5. Cook for another 20-minutes.
6. Set aside for 10-minutes, then slice and serve.

Breakfast Chicken & Bacon Casserole

Prep time: 15 minutes | Cook time: 18 minutes | Serves 6

- 255g ground chicken
- 140g bacon, sliced
- 15g butter
- 1 tablespoon almond flour
- 120ml double cream
- 1 egg
- 170g cheddar cheese, shredded
- 1 teaspoon turmeric
- 1 teaspoon paprika
- ½ teaspoon ground black pepper
- 1 teaspoon sea salt
- ½ yellow onion, diced

1. Grease the inside of the air fryer basket with butter.
2. In a bowl, mix ground chicken with salt and pepper.
3. Add paprika, turmeric and mix well.
4. Add shredded cheese to the mixture.
5. Beat the egg into the ground chicken and mix until well blended.
6. In a small bowl, whisk together the cream and almond flour.
7. Dice the yellow onion.
8. Place the ground chicken mixture into the bottom of the air fryer tray.
9. Sprinkle diced onion and cream mixture on top of the ground chicken.
10. Add layers of bacon and shredded cheese.
11. Preheat the air fryer to 190°C (380°F).
12. Once cooked, allow the casserole to cool for a few minutes before serving.

Turkey & Cheese Calzone

Prep time: 5 minutes | Cook time: 10 minutes | Serves 4

- 1 free-range egg, beaten
- 25g mozzarella cheese, grated
- 100g cheddar cheese, grated
- 28g bacon, diced, cooked
- Cooked turkey, shredded
- 4 tablespoons tomato sauce
- Salt and pepper to taste
- 1 teaspoon thyme
- 1 teaspoon basil
- 1 teaspoon oregano
- 1 package frozen pizza dough

1. Roll the pizza dough out into small circles, the same size as a small pizza.
2. Add thyme, oregano, basil into a bowl with tomato sauce and mix well.
3. Pour a small amount of sauce onto your pizza bases and spread across the surface.
4. Add the turkey, bacon, and cheese.
5. Brush the edge of dough with beaten egg, then fold over and pinch to seal.
6. Brush the outside with more egg.
7. Place into air fryer and cook at 180°C for 10 minutes. Serve warm.

Chapter 6
Beef, Lamb and Pork Recipes

Argentinian Beef Empanadas
Prep time: 5 minutes | Cook time: 23 minutes |Serves 4

- 2 tablespoons (28 g) unsalted butter
- 1 yellow onion, diced
- 1 red bell pepper, diced
- 1 pound (455 g) ground beef
- 11/2 tablespoons (10.5 g) cumin
- 1 tablespoon (7 g) paprika
- 1 teaspoon oregano
- 1 teaspoon kosher salt, plus more for seasoning
- 1/3 cup (50 g) raisins
- 1/2 cup (50 g) green olives, sliced
- 2 hard-boiled eggs, sliced
- Juice of 1 lime
- 1 package (12 ounces, or 340 g) frozen empanada discs, thawed
- Vegetable oil for spraying

1. To make the empanada filling, heat the butter in a large, deep skillet over medium heat. When the butter is foamy, add the onion, season with salt, and sauté for 5 minutes. Add the bell pepper and sauté an additional 3 minutes. Add the ground beef and spices and cook, stirring, until the meat is no longer pink. Remove from the heat. Drain any accumulated fat from the pan. Add the raisins, green olives, and eggs, stir to combine, and allow to cool to room temperature. Add the lime juice and stir to combine. Taste and adjust the seasoning, adding more salt as necessary.
2. Remove 1 of the empanada wrappers from the package and place it on a board. Using a rolling pin, roll the wrapper out in each direction so that it is slightly larger. Place a heaping $1/4$ cup (50 g) of the beef filling on 1 side of the empanada wrapper. Moisten the edges of the wrapper with a little water and fold the wrapper in half to form a half-moon shape. Press the dough closed around the filling and then crimp the edges of the dough with a fork to seal them shut. Place the filled empanada on a baking tray lined with parchment paper. Repeat with the remaing wrappers and filling. (May be refrigerated, covered, at this point for up to several hours.)
3. Preheat the air fryer to 375°F (190°C). Spray the basket of the air fryer and the empanadas with oil. Working in 2 batches, place 5 empanadas in the basket of the air fryer. Cook for 8 minutes, then turn the empanadas over. Cook until the second side is firm and baked, another 5 to 7 minutes. Repeat with the second batch of empanadas. Serve immediately.

Apple Pork Tenderloin
Prep time: 10 minutes | Cook time: 14 to 19 minutes | Serves 4

- 4 pork tenderloin medallions
- 1 tablespoon apple butter
- 2 teaspoons olive oil
- 2 Granny Smith apples or Braeburn apples, sliced
- 3 celery stalks, sliced
- 1 onion, sliced
- 1/2 teaspoon dried thyme
- 1/3 cup apple juice

1. Rub each pork medallion with apple butter and olive oil.
2. In a medium mixing bowl, combine the pork, apples, celery, onion, thyme, and apple juice.
3. Transfer the mixture to the air fryer basket and cook for 14 to 19 minutes, or until the pork reaches at least 63°C on a meat thermometer and the apples and vegetables are tender. Stir once during cooking.
4. Serve immediately.

Spicy Lamb Sirloin Steak
Prep time: 15 minutes | Cooking time: 40 minutes | Serves 4

- 1 teaspoon ground fennel
- 1 teaspoon ground cinnamon
- 1/2 teaspoon Ground Cardamom
- 1/2 onion
- 4 slices ginger
- 5 cloves Garlic
- 1 teaspoon Garam Masala
- 1/2 - 1 teaspoon cayenne
- 1 teaspoon Salt
- lamb sirloin steaks

1. In a food processor, add all the ingredients except for the lamb chops.
2. Pulse and blend until the onion is finely minced and all the ingredients are well combined, about 3-4 minutes.
3. Add the mixed spice paste to the lamb steaks and coat well.
4. Allow the mixture to marinate for 30 minutes or up to 24 hours in the refrigerator.
5. Preheat your air fryer to 170°C (340°F) for 15 minutes and place the lamb steaks in a single layer in the air fryer basket. Cook for 15-20 minutes, flipping halfway through.
6. Using a meat thermometer, ensure that the lamb has reached an internal temperature of 65°C (150°F) for medium well, and serve.

Espresso-Grilled Pork Fillet

Prep time: 15 minutes | Cook time: 9 to 11 minutes | Serves 4

- 1 tablespoon demerara sugar
- 2 teaspoons espresso powder
- 1 teaspoon smoked paprika
- ½ teaspoon dried marjoram
- 1 tablespoon honey
- 1 tablespoon freshly squeezed lemon juice
- 2 teaspoons olive oil
- 1 (450g) pork fillet

1. In a small bowl, mix the demerara sugar, espresso powder, smoked paprika, and marjoram.
2. Stir in the honey, lemon juice, and olive oil until well mixed.
3. Spread the honey mixture over the pork and let stand for 10 minutes at room temperature.
4. Grill the pork fillet in the air fryer basket for 9 to 11 minutes, or until the pork registers at least 63°C on a meat thermometer. Slice the meat to serve.

Pork and Potatoes

Prep time: 5 minutes | Cook time: 25 minutes | Serves 4

- 450g new potatoes, rinsed and dried
- 2 teaspoons olive oil
- 1 (450g) pork tenderloin, cut into 2.5cm cubes
- 1 onion, chopped
- 1 red bell pepper, chopped
- 2 garlic cloves, minced
- ½ teaspoon dried oregano
- 2 tablespoons low-sodium chicken stock

1. In a medium bowl, toss the potatoes and olive oil to coat.
2. Transfer the potatoes to the air fryer basket. Roast for 15 minutes.
3. In a medium metal bowl, mix the potatoes, pork, onion, red bell pepper, garlic, and oregano.
4. Drizzle with the chicken stock. Put the bowl in the air fryer basket. Roast for about 10 minutes more, shaking the basket once during cooking, until the pork reaches at least 63°C on a meat thermometer and the potatoes are tender. Serve immediately.

Blue Cheese Burgers

Prep time: 10 minutes | Cook time:20 minutes |Serves 4

- Rapeseed oil
- 450g lean minced beef
- 75g blue cheese, crumbled
- 1 teaspoon Worcestershire sauce
- ½ teaspoon freshly ground black pepper
- ½ teaspoon hot sauce
- ½ teaspoon minced garlic
- ¼ teaspoon salt
- 4 wholemeal buns

1. Spray a air fryer basket lightly with rapeseed oil.
2. In a large bowl, mix together the minced beef, blue cheese, Worcestershire sauce, black pepper, hot sauce, garlic, and salt.
3. Form the mixture into 4 patties.
4. Place the patties in the air fryer basket in a single layer, leaving a little room between them for even cooking.
5. Air fry at 180°C for 10 minutes. Flip over and air fry until the meat reaches an internal temperature of at least 71°C, an additional 7 to 10 minutes.
6. Place each patty on a bun and serve with low-calorie toppings like sliced tomatoes or onions.

Beef & Mushrooms

Prep time: 5 minutes | Cook time: 10 minutes | Serves 1

- 170g of beef
- ¼ onion, diced
- 2 tablespoons of favorite marinade
- 80g mushroom slices

1. Cut beef strips or cubes and place in a bowl.
2. Coat the meat with marinade and cover bowl.
3. Place in the fridge for about 3-hours.
4. Put the meat into a baking dish and add onion and mushrooms.
5. Air fry at 180°C (350°Fahrenheit) for 10-minutes. Serve warm.

Pork and Fruit Kebabs

Prep time: 15 minutes | Cook time: 9 to 12 minutes | Serves 4

- 80g apricot jam
- 2 tablespoons freshly squeezed lemon juice
- 2 teaspoons olive oil
- ½ teaspoon dried tarragon
- 450g pork tenderloin, cut into 2.5cm cubes
- 4 plums, pitted and quartered
- 4 small apricots, pitted and halved

1. In a large bowl, mix the apricot jam, lemon juice, olive oil, and tarragon.
2. Add the pork and stir to coat. Let stand for 10 minutes at room temperature.
3. Alternating the items, thread the pork, plums, and apricots onto 4 metal skewers that fit into the air fryer. Brush with any remaining jam mixture. Discard any remaining marinade.
4. Grill the kebabs in the air fryer for 9 to 12 minutes, or until the pork reaches 63°C on a meat thermometer and the fruit is tender. Serve immediately.

Steak and Vegetable Kebabs
Prep time: 15 minutes | Cook time: 5 to 7 minutes | Serves 4

- 2 tablespoons balsamic vinegar
- 2 teaspoons olive oil
- ½ teaspoon dried marjoram
- ⅛ teaspoon freshly ground black pepper
- 340g round steak, cut into 2.5cm pieces
- 1 red bell pepper, sliced
- 16 button mushrooms
- 150g cherry tomatoes

1. In a medium bowl, stir together the balsamic vinegar, olive oil, marjoram, and black pepper.
2. Add the steak and stir to coat. Let stand for 10 minutes at room temperature.
3. Alternating items, thread the beef, red bell pepper, mushrooms, and tomatoes onto 8 bamboo or metal skewers that fit in the air fryer.
4. Grill in the air fryer for 5 to 7 minutes, or until the beef is browned and reaches at least 63°C on a meat thermometer. Serve immediately.

Easy Air-Fried Pork Chops
Prep time: 5 minutes | Cook time: 15 minutes | Serves 2

- 2 pork chops
- 60g breadcrumbs
- 1 tablespoon olive oil
- 1 egg, beaten
- 1 tablespoon ground almonds
- Salt and pepper to taste

1. Season pork chops with salt and pepper.
2. Add ground almonds to a mixing bowl.
3. In another small bowl, add beaten egg.
4. In a third bowl, combine breadcrumbs with olive oil.
5. Coat the pork chops with ground almonds, dip in egg, and coat with breadcrumbs.
6. Place chops into air fryer basket and cook at 200°C for 10-minutes.
7. Flip chops over and cook on the other side for an additional 5-minutes. Serve warm.

Hawaiian Pork Sliders

Prep time: 15 minutes | Cook time:15 minutes |Serves 4

- Olive oil
- 120g crushed pineapple, drained
- 450g lean ground pork
- 1 teaspoon Worcestershire sauce
- ½ teaspoon garlic powder
- ½ teaspoon salt
- ½ teaspoon freshly ground black pepper
- Pinch of cayenne pepper
- 8 wholemeal slider buns

1. Lightly grease the air fryer basket with olive oil.
2. In a large bowl, mix together the crushed pineapple, ground pork, Worcestershire sauce, garlic powder, salt, black pepper, and cayenne pepper.
3. Form the mixture into 8 small patties.
4. Place the patties in the air fryer basket in a single layer and lightly spray with olive oil. You may need to cook them in batches.
5. Air fry for 7 minutes. Flip the patties over, lightly spray with olive oil, and cook until the patties reach an internal temperature of at least 70°C, an additional 5 to 8 minutes.
6. Place the cooked patties on the slider buns and serve.

Pub Burger

Prep time: 10 minutes | Cooking time: 30 minutes | Serves 4

- 8 large leaves of gem lettuce
- 450g ground beef
- 4 bacon-wrapped onion rings
- 120ml full-fat mayonnaise
- 8 slices of pickles
- 2 tbsp melted salted butter
- 2 tsp sriracha
- 1/4 tsp garlic powder
- 1/2 tsp salt
- 1/4 tsp black pepper

1. In a medium bowl, combine the ground beef, salt, and pepper. Form into four patties.
2. Brush each patty with melted butter and place into the air fryer basket. Adjust the temperature to 190°C and set the timer for 10 minutes.
3. Flip the patties halfway through the cooking time for a medium burger. Add an additional 3-5 minutes for well-done.
4. In a small bowl, mix together the mayonnaise, sriracha, and garlic powder. Set aside.
5. Place each cooked burger on a gem lettuce leaf and top with an onion ring, two slices of pickles, and a dollop of the prepared burger sauce.
6. Wrap another gem lettuce leaf tightly around the burger to hold. Serve warm.

Crunchy Back Bacon

Prep time: 5 minutes | Cook time: 10 minutes | Serves 4

- 10-ounces back bacon, sliced
- 1 teaspoon double cream
- ½ teaspoon salt
- ¼ teaspoon freshly ground black pepper
- ½ teaspoon ground coriander
- ½ teaspoon ground thyme

1. In a mixing bowl combine the thyme, coriander, black pepper, and salt.
2. Sprinkle this spice mix on top of the bacon slices on each side.
3. Preheat your air fryer to 180°C / 360°F.
4. Place prepared bacon inside the air fryer and cook it for 5 minutes.
5. After this turn, the sliced bacon over and cook for an additional 5 minutes.
6. Once the bacon is cooked, remove it from the air fryer and sprinkle it with double cream and serve immediately!

Bacon Omelet

Prep time: 5 minutes | Cook time: 13 minutes | Serves 6

- 6 large free-range eggs
- 1 teaspoon butter
- 115g streaky bacon
- 1 tablespoon dried dill
- ½ teaspoon salt
- ½ teaspoon turmeric
- 60ml almond milk

1. In a mixing bowl, whisk the eggs and add the almond milk.
2. Mix in the dried dill, salt, and turmeric.
3. Thinly slice the bacon.
4. Preheat your air fryer to 180°C (356°F) and place the bacon in the air fryer basket tray.
5. Cook the bacon for 5 minutes.
6. Turn the bacon over and pour the egg mixture on top of it.
7. Cook the omelette for 8 minutes.
8. When the omelette is cooked, transfer it to a plate and slice into servings. Serve hot.

Crumbed Pork & Semi-Dried Tomato Pesto

Prep time: 15 minutes | Cook time: 20 minutes | Serves 2

- 120ml milk
- 1 egg
- 100g breadcrumbs
- 1 tablespoon parmesan cheese, grated
- ¼ bunch of thyme, chopped
- 1 teaspoon pine nuts
- 40g semi-dried tomatoes
- 60g almond flour
- 2 pork cutlets
- 1 lemon, zested
- Sea salt and black pepper to taste
- 6 basil leaves
- 1 tablespoon olive oil

1. In a bowl, combine and whisk together the milk and egg, then set aside.
2. In another bowl, mix together the breadcrumbs, grated parmesan, thyme, lemon zest, salt, and pepper.
3. Add the almond flour to another bowl.
4. Dip each pork cutlet first into the almond flour, then into the egg and milk mixture, and finally into the breadcrumb mixture.
5. Preheat the air fryer to 180°C/360°F.
6. Spray the air fryer basket with cooking spray.
7. Set the air fryer timer to 20 minutes.
8. Place the pork inside the basket and cook until golden and crisp.
9. Prepare the pesto: add the semi-dried tomatoes, pine nuts, olive oil, and basil leaves into a food processor.
10. Blend for 20 seconds.
11. When the pork is ready, serve with the pesto and a salad of your choice.

Crispy Alfredo Beef

Prep time: 5 minutes | Cook time: 15 minutes | Serves 4

- 1 tablespoon extra-virgin olive oil
- Salt and pepper to taste
- 6 tablespoons breadcrumbs
- 1 jar (16-ounces) Alfredo pasta sauce
- 1 lb. beef fillet

1. Cut your beef fillet into 1-inch cubes, then transfer to mixing bowl, coat with pasta sauce.
2. In another mixing bowl, mix breadcrumbs, salt, pepper, and oil.
3. Coat beef cubes with the breadcrumb mixture.
4. Preheat your air fryer to 380°Celsius and cook for 15-minutes, stirring occasionally. Serve hot!

Pork Loin with Potatoes & Herbs

Prep time: 5 minutes | Cook time: 25 minutes | Serves 2

- 900g pork loin
- 1/2 teaspoon garlic powder
- 1/2 teaspoon red pepper flakes
- 1/2 teaspoon black pepper
- 2 large potatoes, cut into chunks
- Salt, to taste
- Chopped parsley, to taste

1. Sprinkle the pork loin with garlic powder, red pepper flakes, salt, black pepper, and parsley.
2. Preheat your air fryer to 190°C/375°F and place pork loin and potatoes to one side in the basket of the air fryer.
3. Cook for 25 minutes or until the pork loin is cooked through.
4. Remove the pork loin and potatoes from the air fryer.
5. Allow the pork loin to cool before slicing and serving. Enjoy!

Beef Roll-Up
Prep time: 5 minutes | Cook time: 14 minutes | Serves 4

- 900g beef flank steak
- Salt and pepper to taste
- 75g baby spinach, fresh
- 85g roasted red bell peppers
- 6 slices provolone cheese
- 3 tablespoons Pesto

1. Open the steak and spread the pesto evenly over the meat.
2. Layer the cheese, roasted red peppers and spinach ¾ of the way down the meat.
3. Roll up and secure with toothpicks.
4. Season with sea salt and pepper.
5. Preheat air fryer to 200°C (400°F).
6. Place the roll-ups in the fry basket and into the air fryer and cook it for 14 minutes.
7. Halfway through the cook time, rotate the meat.
8. When the cook time is completed, allow the meat to rest for 10 minutes before cutting and serving.

Country Style Ribs
Prep time: 5 minutes | Cook time: 12 minutes | Serves 4

- 4 country-style pork ribs, trimmed of excess fat
- Salt and black pepper to taste
- 1 teaspoon dried marjoram
- 1 teaspoon garlic powder
- 1 teaspoon thyme
- 2 teaspoons dry mustard
- 3 tablespoons coconut oil
- 3 tablespoons cornstarch

1. Preheat the air fryer to 200°Celsius for 2 minutes.
2. Place ingredients in a bowl, except pork ribs.
3. Soak the ribs in the mixture and rub in.
4. Place the ribs into air fryer for 12-minutes. Serve and enjoy!

Air Fryer Apple Pork Balls
Prep time: 5 minutes | Cook time: 15 minutes | Serves 8

- 2 teaspoons wholegrain mustard
- 5 basil leaves, chopped
- Salt and pepper to taste
- 2 tablespoons cheddar cheese, grated
- 4 garlic cloves, minced
- 1 small apple, chopped
- 1 large onion, chopped
- 1 lb. pork mince

1. Add the pork mince, onion, and apple into mixing bowl and stir.
2. Add mustard, honey, garlic, cheese, basil, pepper, salt and mix well.
3. Make small balls from mixture and place them inside of air fryer basket.
4. Cook at 200°C for 15-minutes.

Beef & Potato

Prep time: 5 minutes | Cook time: 20 minutes | Serves 4

- 2 eggs
- 680g mashed potatoes
- 450g ground beef
- 2 tablespoons garlic powder
- 240ml sour cream
- Pinch of salt
- Black pepper to taste

1. Preheat your air fryer to 200°C (390°F).
2. Add all the ingredients into a bowl.
3. Place ingredients in a heat safe dish and cook for 20 minutes. Serve warm.

Spicy Grilled Steak

Prep time: 7 minutes | Cook time: 6 to 9 minutes | Serves 4

- 2 tablespoons low-sodium salsa
- 1 tablespoon minced chipotle pepper
- 1 tablespoon apple cider vinegar
- 1 teaspoon ground cumin
- ⅛ teaspoon freshly ground black pepper
- ⅛ teaspoon chilli flakes
- ¾ pound sirloin tip steak, cut into 4 pieces and gently pounded to about ⅓ inch thick

1. In a small bowl, thoroughly mix the salsa, chipotle pepper, cider vinegar, cumin, black pepper, and chilli flakes. Rub this mixture into both sides of each steak piece. Let stand for 15 minutes at room temperature.
2. Grill the steaks in the air fryer, two at a time, for 6 to 9 minutes, or until they reach at least 63°C on a meat thermometer.
3. Remove the steaks to a clean plate and cover with aluminium foil to keep warm. Repeat with the remaining steaks.
4. Slice the steaks thinly against the grain and serve.

Cheese Burgers

Prep time: 5 minutes | Cook time: 11 minutes | Serves 6

- 450g minced beef
- 6 slices of cheddar cheese
- Salt and pepper to taste
- 6 burger buns

1. Preheat the air fryer to 180°C (350°F).
2. Divide the minced beef into six portions and shape them into patties. Season with salt and pepper.
3. Place the patties in the air fryer basket and cook for 10 minutes.
4. After 10 minutes, place a slice of cheese on each patty and cook for an additional minute until melted.
5. Meanwhile, toast the burger buns in the air fryer for 1-2 minutes.
6. Assemble the cheeseburgers with the patties and buns. Serve hot.

Yummy Rib-Eye Steak

Prep time: 5 minutes | Cook time: 21 minutes | Serves 4

- 1 (900 g) ribeye steak
- 1 tablespoon of steak rub
- 1 tablespoon olive oil

1. Preheat your air fryer to 200°C for 4-minutes.
2. Season both sides of steak with steak rub and olive oil.
3. Place seasoned steak in air fryer basket and cook for 14-minutes.
4. Turn over the steak and cook on the other side for an additional 7-minutes. Serve hot!

Simple Air-Fried Steak

Prep time: 5 minutes | Cook time: 6 minutes | Serves 1

- 1 (3cm) thick beef steak
- Salt and freshly ground black pepper to taste
- Cooking spray

1. Preheat your air fryer to 200°C (400°F) for 5 minutes.
2. Season the beef steak with salt and freshly ground black pepper.
3. Spray the beef steak with cooking spray.
4. Cook the beef steak in the preheated air fryer for 3 minutes.
5. Flip the steak and cook for an additional 3 minutes on the other side.
6. Serve hot.

Chapter 7
Fish and Seafood Recipes

Maryland-Style Crab Cakes
Prep time: 40 minutes | Cook time:15 minutes |Serves 6

- 4 (170g) cans lump crab meat, drained
- 100g whole-wheat breadcrumbs
- 1 cup chopped fresh parsley
- 4 cloves garlic, minced
- 4 teaspoons Dijon mustard
- 2 teaspoons seafood seasoning (such as Old Bay)
- 2 large eggs, beaten
- Olive oil

1. In a large bowl, mix together the crab meat, breadcrumbs, parsley, garlic, Dijon mustard, and seafood seasoning. Add the eggs and stir to combine. Cover the bowl and refrigerate for 30 minutes.
2. Preheat the oven to 200°C/180°C fan/gas mark 6.
3. Form the mixture into 12 crab cakes and place them on a lightly oiled baking tray.
4. Bake the crab cakes for 15 minutes, until golden brown and crispy.
5. Serve the crab cakes hot, garnished with a sprig of parsley or a slice of lemon.

Crispy Herbed Salmon
Prep time: 5 minutes | Cook time: 9 to 12 minutes| Serves 4

- 4 (6-ounce) skinless salmon fillets
- 3 tablespoons honey mustard
- ½ teaspoon dried thyme
- ½ teaspoon dried basil
- ¼ cup panko bread crumbs
- ⅓ cup crushed potato chips
- 2 tablespoons olive oil

1. Place the salmon on a plate. In a small bowl, combine the mustard, thyme, and basil, and spread evenly over the salmon.
2. In another small bowl, combine the bread crumbs and potato chips and mix well. Drizzle in the olive oil and mix until combined.
3. Place the salmon in the air fryer basket and gently but firmly press the bread crumb mixture onto the top of each fillet.
4. Air fry for 9 to 12 minutes or until the salmon reaches at least 63°C on a meat thermometer and the topping is browned and crisp.

Fish and Chips

Prep time: 25 minutes | Cook time:35 minutes |Serves 4

- 1 tablespoon vegetable oil, plus more for spraying
- 2 large floury potatoes, scrubbed and peeled
- 1 teaspoon salt
- ½ teaspoon freshly ground black pepper
- Vegetable oil
- 4 (120g) cod fillets
- 1½ teaspoons salt, divided, plus more as needed
- 1½ teaspoons black pepper, divided, plus more as needed
- ½ cup plain flour
- 2 eggs
- 1½ cups breadcrumbs
- ¼ teaspoon cayenne pepper

1. Preheat the oven to 220°C/200°C fan/gas mark 7. Spray a baking tray with vegetable oil.
2. Cut the potatoes into thick chips, about 1 cm wide. Place them in a bowl of cold water for 10 minutes, then drain and pat dry with kitchen paper.
3. In a large bowl, mix together the oil, salt, and pepper and toss with the potatoes to coat.
4. Place the potatoes on the prepared baking tray in a single layer. Bake for 30-35 minutes, turning occasionally, until golden brown and crispy. Set aside and keep warm.
5. Spray the fryer basket with vegetable oil.
6. Season the fillets with salt and black pepper.
7. In a shallow bowl, mix together the plain flour, ½ teaspoon of salt, and ½ teaspoon of black pepper.
8. In a second bowl, whisk together the eggs, 1 teaspoon of water, and a pinch of salt and pepper.
9. In another shallow bowl, combine the breadcrumbs, cayenne pepper, and remaining 1 teaspoon of salt and 1 teaspoon of black pepper.
10. Coat each fillet in the seasoned flour, then coat with the egg, and dredge in the breadcrumb mixture.
11. Place the fillets in the fryer basket in a single layer. Lightly spray the fish with vegetable oil. You may need to cook them in batches.
12. Air fry for 8 to 10 minutes. Turn the fillets over and lightly spray with vegetable oil. Cook until golden brown and crispy, 5 to 10 more minutes.
13. Serve the fish and chips hot, garnished with a slice of lemon and accompanied by tartar sauce or mushy peas, if desired.

Prawn and Green Beans

Prep time: 5 minutes | Cooking time: 15 minutes | Serves 4

- 450g Prawn, peeled and deveined
- A pinch of salt and black pepper
- 225g green beans, trimmed and halved
- Juice of 1 lime
- 2 tablespoons coriander, chopped
- 60g clarified butter, melted

1. In a pan that fits your air fryer, mix all the ingredients, place in the air fryer and cook at 180°C for 15 minutes shaking the air fryer halfway.
2. Divide into bowls and serve.

Air-Fried Crab Herb Croquettes
Prep time: 15 minutes | Cook time: 18 minutes | Serves 6

- 450g crab meat
- 100g breadcrumbs
- 2 egg whites
- Salt and black pepper to taste
- 1/2 teaspoon chopped parsley
- 1/4 teaspoon chopped chives
- 1/4 teaspoon chopped tarragon
- 2 tablespoons chopped celery
- 4 tablespoons mayonnaise
- 4 tablespoons reduced-fat sour cream
- 1 teaspoon olive oil
- 1/2 teaspoon lime juice
- 120g red pepper, chopped
- 60g onion, chopped

1. Preheat your air fryer to 180°C.
2. In a bowl, mix the breadcrumbs with salt and pepper.
3. In another small bowl, add the egg whites.
4. In a separate bowl, add all the remaining ingredients and mix well.
5. Form the crab mixture into croquettes and dip each one into the egg whites, and then into the breadcrumbs.
6. Place the croquettes into the air fryer and cook for 18 minutes.

Asian Steamed Tuna
Prep time: 10 minutes| Cook time: 8 to 10 minutes | Serves 4

- 4 small tuna steaks
- 2 tablespoons low-sodium soy sauce
- 2 teaspoons sesame oil
- 2 teaspoons rice vinegar
- 1 teaspoon grated fresh ginger
- 1/8 teaspoon ground black pepper
- 1 stalk lemongrass, bent in half
- 3 tablespoons lemon juice

1. Place the tuna steaks on a plate.
2. In a small bowl, combine the soy sauce, sesame oil, rice vinegar, and ginger. Mix well and pour the mixture over the tuna. Marinate for 10 minutes, gently rubbing the mixture into both sides of the tuna. Sprinkle with black pepper.
3. Place the lemongrass in a steamer basket and place the tuna on top of it. Pour lemon juice and 1 tablespoon of water in the bottom of the steamer.
4. Steam the fish for 8 to 10 minutes or until the tuna registers at least 63°C (145°F) using a meat thermometer. Discard the lemongrass and serve the tuna.

Cajun Salmon

Prep time: 5 minutes | Cook time: 7 minutes | Serves 1

- 1 salmon fillet
- Cajun seasoning
- Juice of half a lemon, to serve

1. Preheat your air fryer to 180°C (355°F).
2. Sprinkle Cajun seasoning all over the salmon fillet.
3. Place the salmon fillet on a grill pan, skin side down, and cook in the air fryer for 7 minutes.
4. Squeeze the juice of half a lemon over the cooked salmon and serve immediately.

Scallops and Spring Veggies

Prep time: 10 minutes| Cook time: 7 to 10 minutes| Serves 4

- 225g asparagus, ends trimmed, cut into 5cm pieces
- 150g sugar snap peas
- 450g sea scallops
- 1 tablespoon lemon juice
- 2 teaspoons olive oil
- ½ teaspoon dried thyme
- Pinch salt
- Freshly ground black pepper

1. Place the asparagus and sugar snap peas in the air fryer basket. Cook for 2 to 3 minutes or until the vegetables are just starting to get tender.
2. Meanwhile, check the scallops for a small muscle attached to the side, and pull it off and discard.
3. In a medium bowl, toss the scallops with the lemon juice, olive oil, thyme, salt, and pepper. Place into the air fryer basket on top of the vegetables.
4. Steam for 5 to 7 minutes, tossing the basket once during cooking time, until the scallops are just firm when tested with your finger and are opaque in the center, and the vegetables are tender. Serve immediately.

Calamari with Tomato Sauce

Prep time: 5 minutes | Cook time: 8 minutes | Serves 4

FOR THE SAUCE:

- 1 lb. fresh whole tomatoes, diced
- 1 stalk of celery, chopped
- 1/2 green bell pepper, diced
- 1/2 cup onion, chopped
- 3 cloves garlic, minced
- 1 tablespoon olive oil
- Salt and pepper to taste

FOR THE CALAMARI:

- 3 lbs. calamari, cleaned and sliced into 1/2-inch rings
- 1/3 cup olive oil
- 1 tablespoon fresh oregano, chopped
- 1 teaspoon lemon juice
- 1 tablespoon garlic, minced
- 1/4 teaspoon chopped fresh lemon peel
- 1/4 teaspoon crushed red pepper
- 1/4 cup vinegar

1. Preheat the air fryer to 400°F (200°C).
2. To make the sauce, heat the olive oil in a saucepan over medium heat. Add the celery, green pepper, onion, and garlic and cook until the vegetables are tender, about 5 minutes. Add the diced tomatoes and salt and pepper to taste. Cook until the tomatoes are softened and the sauce has thickened, about 10 minutes. Remove from heat and set aside.
3. In a large bowl, combine the calamari, olive oil, oregano, lemon juice, garlic, lemon peel, crushed red pepper, and vinegar. Toss to coat the calamari evenly.
4. Place the calamari in the air fryer basket and cook for 6 minutes. Stir once, then cook for an additional 2 to 4 minutes, or until the calamari is crispy and cooked through.
5. Serve the calamari hot with the tomato sauce on the side for dipping.

Baja Fish Tacos

Prep time: 5 minutes | Cook time: 10 minutes | Serves 4

- 1 pound (455 g) tilapia fillets (or other mild white fish)
- 1/2 cup (63 g) all-purpose flour
- 1 teaspoon garlic powder
- 1 teaspoon kosher salt
- 1/4 teaspoon cayenne pepper
- 1/2 cup (115 g) mayonnaise
- 3 tablespoons (45 ml) milk
- 13/4 cups (89 g) panko bread crumbs
- Vegetable oil for spraying
- 8 corn tortillas
- 1/4 head red or green cabbage, shredded
- 1 ripe avocado, halved and each half cut into 4 slices
- 12 ounces (340 g) pico de gallo or other fresh salsa
- Mexican crema
- 1 lime, cut into wedges

1. To make the fish, cut the fish fillets into strips 3 to 4 inches (7.5 to 10 cm) long and 1 inch (2.5 cm) wide. Combine the flour, garlic powder, salt, and cayenne pepper on a plate and whisk to combine. In a shallow bowl, whisk the mayonnaise and milk together. Place the panko on a separate plate. Dredge the fish strips in the seasoned flour, shaking off any excess. Dip the strips in the mayonnaise mixture, coating them completely, then dredge in the panko, shaking off any excess. Place the fish strips on a plate or rack.
2. Working in batches, spray half the fish strips with oil and arrange them in the basket of the air fryer, taking care not to crowd them. Cook at 400°F (200°C) for 4 minutes, then flip and cook for another 3 to 4 minutes until the outside is brown and crisp and the inside is opaque and flakes easily with a fork. Repeat with the remaining strips.
3. Heat the tortillas in the microwave or on the stovetop. To assemble the tacos, place 2 fish strips inside each tortilla. Top with shredded cabbage, a slice of avocado, pico de gallo, and a dollop of crema. Serve with a lime wedge on the side.

Sesame Prawn

Prep time: 3 minutes | Cooking time: 12 minutes | Serves 4

- 450g Prawn
- A pinch of salt and black pepper
- 1 tablespoon sesame seeds, toasted
- ½ teaspoon mixed herbs
- olive oil

1. In a bowl, mix the Prawn with the rest of the ingredients and toss well.
2. Put the Prawn in the air fryer's basket, cook at 190°C for 12 minutes, divide into bowls and serve.

Cajun-Seasoned Lemon Salmon

Prep time: 5 minutes | Cook time: 7 minutes | Serves 1

- 1 salmon fillet
- 1 teaspoon Cajun seasoning
- 2 lemon wedges, for serving
- 1 teaspoon liquid stevia
- ½ lemon, juiced

1. Preheat your air fryer to 180°C (350°F).
2. Combine lemon juice and liquid stevia and coat salmon with this mixture.
3. Sprinkle Cajun seasoning all over salmon.
4. Place salmon on parchment paper in air fryer and cook for 7-minutes.
5. Serve with lemon wedges.

Snapper Scampi

Prep time: 5 minutes | Cook time: 8 to 10 minutes | Serves 4

- 4 (6-ounce) skinless snapper or arctic char fillets
- 1 tablespoon olive oil
- 3 tablespoons lemon juice, divided
- ½ teaspoon dried basil
- Pinch of salt
- Freshly ground black pepper
- 2 tablespoons unsalted butter
- 2 cloves garlic, minced

1. Rub the fish fillets with olive oil and 1 tablespoon of the lemon juice. Sprinkle with the basil, salt, and pepper, and place in the air fryer basket.
2. Grill the fish for 7 to 8 minutes or until the fish just flakes when tested with a fork. Remove the fish from the basket and put on a serving plate. Cover to keep warm.
3. In a 6-by-6-by-2-inch pan, combine the butter, remaining 2 tablespoons lemon juice, and garlic. Cook in the air fryer for 1 to 2 minutes or until the garlic is sizzling. Pour this mixture over the fish and serve.

Coconut Prawn
Prep time: 5 minutes | Cook time: 10 minutes | Serves 4

- 1 cup panko breadcrumbs
- 1 cup unsweetened desiccated coconut
- 1 cup almond flour
- Sea salt to taste
- 2 lbs. prawns
- 1 cup egg whites

1. In a mixing bowl, combine desiccated coconut and panko breadcrumbs.
2. Season lightly with sea salt.
3. In another bowl, add almond flour, and in a third bowl, add egg whites.
4. Preheat your air fryer to 170°C (340°F).
5. Dip each prawn into the almond flour, egg whites, then the breadcrumb and coconut mixture.
6. Cook the prawns in the air fryer for 10 minutes, turning them over halfway through cooking.
7. Serve with your preferred dipping sauce.

Garlic Salmon Patties
Prep time: 5 minutes | Cook time: 15 minutes | Serves 4

- 1 egg
- 14-ounce can of salmon, drained
- Salt and pepper to taste
- 2 tablespoons mayonnaise
- ½ teaspoon garlic powder
- 4 tablespoons onion, minced
- 4 tablespoons gluten-free flour
- 4 tablespoons cornmeal

1. Add drained salmon into a bowl, and with a fork flake the salmon.
2. Add garlic powder, mayonnaise, flour, cornmeal, onion, egg, pepper, and salt.
3. Mix well.
4. Make round patties with mix and place them in the air fryer.
5. Air fry at 150°C for 15-minutes.

Grilled Prawns

Prep time: 5 minutes | Cook time: 15 minutes | Serves 4

- 8 medium prawns
- Salt and pepper to taste
- 3 garlic cloves, minced
- 15g butter, melted
- 1 sprig of rosemary

1. Add ingredients to a bowl and toss well.
2. Add the marinated prawns to air fryer basket and cook at 150°C for 7 minutes.
3. Serve hot!

Air-Fried Cajun Prawn

Prep time: 5 minutes | Cook time: 5 minutes | Serves 4

- 500g Prawns, peeled and deveined
- Pinch of salt
- 1 teaspoon paprika
- 1 tablespoon olive oil
- Pinch of cayenne pepper
- 1 teaspoon Old Bay seasoning

1. Preheat air fryer to 200°C/400°F.
2. In a mixing bowl, combine the prawns, salt, paprika, olive oil, cayenne pepper, and Old Bay seasoning.
3. Place the seasoned prawns into the air fryer basket and cook for 5 minutes.
4. Serve hot.

Chapter 8
Vegetables and Side Dishes

Crispy Breaded Bell Pepper Strips

Prep time: 15 minutes | Cook time:7 minutes |Serves 4

- Olive oil
- 110g whole-wheat panko bread crumbs
- ½ teaspoon paprika
- ½ teaspoon garlic powder
- ½ teaspoon salt
- 1 egg, beaten
- 2 red, orange, or yellow bell peppers, cut into 1.25cm-thick slices

1. Lightly spray an air fryer basket with olive oil.
2. In a medium shallow bowl, mix together the panko bread crumbs, paprika, garlic powder, and salt.
3. In a separate small shallow bowl, whisk the egg with 1½ teaspoons of water to make an egg wash.
4. Dip the bell pepper slices in the egg wash to coat, then dredge them in the panko bread crumbs until evenly coated.
5. Place the bell pepper slices in the air fryer basket in a single layer. Lightly spray the bell pepper strips with oil. You may need to cook these in batches.
6. Air fry until lightly browned, 4 to 7 minutes.
7. Carefully remove from air fryer basket to ensure that the coating does not come off. Serve immediately.

Stuffed Mushrooms

Prep time: 15 minutes | Cook time:10 minutes |Serves 3

- 225g (8oz) chestnut mushrooms
- 75g (½ cup) cooked brown rice
- 3 tbsp vegan cream cheese
- 2 tbsp chopped sun-dried tomatoes, packed in oil, drained
- 3 tbsp chopped fresh parsley
- 2 garlic cloves, finely chopped
- 4 tsp olive oil, divided, plus more
- 45g (½ cup) panko breadcrumbs, divided
- kosher salt
- freshly ground black pepper

1. Preheat the air fryer to 180°C (360°F).
2. Remove the stems from the mushrooms and roughly chop them. In a large bowl, combine the stems, rice, cream cheese, tomatoes, parsley, garlic, 2 teaspoons of olive oil, and ¼ cup of breadcrumbs.
3. Drizzle the insides of the mushroom caps with olive oil. Season with salt and pepper. Spoon the rice mixture into the mushrooms and sprinkle the remaining ¼ cup of breadcrumbs over the top. Drizzle the remaining 2 teaspoons of olive oil over the breadcrumbs.
4. Place the mushrooms in the air fryer basket and cook until the tops are golden and crispy, about 10 minutes.
5. Transfer the mushrooms to a platter and allow to cool slightly before serving.

Onion Rings
Prep time: 10 minutes | Cook time:20 minutes |Serves 2

- 1 large sweet onion
- 1 cup plain flour
- 1 cup aquafaba (from a 15oz [420g] can of chickpeas)
- 2 cups panko breadcrumbs
- 1 tsp smoked paprika
- 1 tsp kosher salt

1. Set the air fryer temperature to 180°C.
2. Slice the onion into 4 thick slices and separate into 18 total rings.
3. Place the flour, aquafaba, and breadcrumbs in three separate medium bowls. Season each bowl with an equal amount of paprika and salt.
4. Dredge the onion rings in the flour, then the aquafaba, followed by the breadcrumbs.
5. Working in batches, place 9 rings in the fryer basket and cook until golden brown and tender, about 10 minutes.
6. Transfer the onion rings to a plate and serve immediately.

Caribbean Yuca Fries
Prep time: 5 minutes | Cook time: 25 minutes |Serves 4

- 3 yuca roots (also known as cassava)
- Vegetable oil for spraying
- 1 teaspoon kosher salt

1. Trim the ends off the yuca roots and cut each one into 2 or 3 pieces depending on the length. Have a bowl of water ready. Peel off the rough outer skin with a paring knife or sharp vegetable peeler. Halve each piece of yuca lengthwise. Place the peeled pieces in a bowl of water to prevent them from oxidizing and turning brown.
2. Fill a large pot with water and bring to a boil over high heat. Season well with salt. Add the yuca pieces to the water and cook until they are tender enough to be pierced with a fork, but not falling apart, approximately 12 to 15 minutes. Drain. Some of the yuca pieces will have fibrous string running down the center. Remove it. Cut the yuca into 2 or 3 pieces to resemble thick-cut french fries.
3. Working in batches, arrange the yuca fries in a single layer in the air fryer basket. Spray with oil. Cook at 400°F (200°C) for 10 minutes, turning the fries halfway through, until the outside of the fries is crisp and browned and the inside fluffy. Repeat with the remaining fries. Spray the cooked yuca with oil and toss with 1 teaspoon salt.
4. Serve the yuca fries warm with Toum, Chipotle Ketchup, or Mint Chimichurri.

Spicy Maple-Soy Brussels Sprouts
Prep time: 5 minutes | Cook time: 27 minutes |Serves 4

- 1/2 pounds (680 g) Brussels sprouts, trimmed and, if large, halved
- 1 tablespoon (15 ml) extra-virgin olive oil
- 1/2 teaspoon kosher salt
- 3 tablespoons (45 ml) soy sauce
- 2 tablespoons (40 g) maple syrup
- Juice and zest of 1 lime
- 1 clove garlic, minced
- 1 tablespoon (15 ml) sriracha

1. Toss the Brussels sprouts with the olive oil and salt. Working in batches if necessary, arrange the sprouts in a single layer in the basket of the air fryer. Cook at 375°F (190°C) until browned, crispy, and fork-tender, 15 to 20 minutes.
2. While the Brussels sprouts are cooking, combine the soy sauce, maple syrup, lime zest and juice, garlic, and sriracha in a small saucepan. Bring to a boil over medium heat. Reduce the heat and simmer until thickened and slightly syrupy, 5 to 7 minutes.
3. Remove the Brussels sprouts from the air fryer. (If you were not able to fit all the Brussels sprouts in the air fryer, cook the remaining Brussels sprouts in the same manner.) Place the Brussels sprouts in a serving bowl and drizzle the maple-soy sauce over them. Stir to coat the sprouts with the sauce and serve warm.

Tempura Shishito Peppers
Prep time: 5 minutes | Cook time: 10 minutes |Serves 4

- 1 cup (125 g) all-purpose flour
- 1/2 cup (64 g) cornstarch
- 2 teaspoons baking soda
- 1 teaspoon kosher salt
- 1 cup (240 ml) seltzer water or club soda
- 8 ounces (225 g) shishito peppers
- Vegetable oil for spraying

1. To make the tempura batter, whisk together the flour, cornstarch, baking soda, and salt in a large bowl. Slowly whisk in the seltzer water until you have created a thick batter. Place a cooling rack over a board lined with wax or parchment paper. Using the stem as handle, dip a shishito pepper in the batter then tap it against the side of the bowl several times to remove any excess. Place the battered peppers on the rack. Repeat with half the peppers, waiting to batter the other half.
2. Brush the basket of the air fryer lightly with oil to prevent sticking. Arrange the battered peppers in a single layer in the air fryer basket. Spray the peppers with oil. Cook at 350°F (180°C) or 7 to 8 minutes until the peppers are browned on the outside and tender on the inside. (Do not be alarmed if you hear the peppers popping in the air fryer. This is normal.) While the first batch of peppers is cooking, batter the remaining peppers.
3. Remove the first batch of peppers from the air fryer and place on a serving plate or platter. Cook the second batch of peppers in the same manner as the first. Serve the peppers warm.

Summer by the Beach Vegetable Patties
Prep time: 10 minutes | Cook time:15 minutes |Serves 4

- 1 (15.5-oz [439-g]) can white beans (cannellini, navy, etc.), liquid reserved for aquafaba
- 1 cup (170 g) shredded zucchini
- 1 cup (99 g) shredded carrots
- 1 cup (142 g) corn kernels
- 1 tsp (2 g) celery seeds
- ¾ tsp salt, or to taste
- ½ tsp tarragon
- ½ tsp cayenne powder
- ½ tsp paprika
- ¼ tsp ground black pepper
- ⅛ tsp dry mustard powder
- ⅛ tsp ground allspice
- ½ cup (60 g) panko breadcrumbs (*use gluten-free)

1. Mash the beans in a large mixing bowl. Place the zucchini and carrot into a strainer and press the liquid out. You just need to get most of it, so don't worry if you don't get every drop.
2. Mix the zucchini, carrots, corn kernels, celery seeds, salt, tarragon, cayenne, paprika, black pepper, mustard powder and allspice into the mashed beans.
3. Add the breadcrumbs to a flat dish. Make patties with ¼ cup (60 ml) of the mixture and then place into the breadcrumbs. Pat the breadcrumbs onto the patties so they will stay on.
4. Place however many patties fit into your air fryer basket. Cook on 350°F (177°C) for 10 minutes, then carefully flip and cook 5 minutes more.
5. Repeat until all the patties are cooked. Serve as is, topped with tartar sauce or on a sandwich.

Tasty Tofu
Prep time: 5 minutes | Cook time: 12 minutes | Serves 4

- 35g cornmeal
- 425g extra firm tofu, drained, cubed
- Salt and pepper to taste
- 1 teaspoon chili flakes
- 90g cornflour

1. Line the air fryer basket with aluminium foil and brush with oil.
2. Preheat your air fryer to 190°C (370°F).
3. Mix all ingredients in a bowl.
4. Place in air fryer and cook for 12 minutes.

Avocado Fries
Prep time: 5 minutes | Cook time: 10 minutes | Serves 4

- 30ml Aquafina
- 1 avocado, sliced
- ½ teaspoon salt
- 50g panko breadcrumbs

1. Toss the panko breadcrumbs and salt together in a bowl.
2. Pour Aquafina into another bowl.
3. Dredge the avocado slices in Aquafina and then panko breadcrumbs.
4. Arrange the slices in single layer in air fryer basket.
5. Air fry at 200°C for 10-minutes.

Carrots with Cumin

Prep time: 5 minutes | Cook time: 12 minutes | Serves 4

- 450g carrots, peeled and chopped
- 15g coriander
- 15ml olive oil
- 1 teaspoon cumin

1. Toss the carrots with cumin and oil.
2. Cook in the air fryer at 200°C for 12 minutes.
3. Sprinkle with coriander over the carrots. Serve and enjoy!

Crispy & Crunchy Baby Corn

Prep time: 5 minutes | Cook time: 10 minutes | Serves 4

- 120g plain flour
- 1 teaspoon garlic powder
- ¼ teaspoon chili powder
- 4 baby corns, boiled
- Salt to taste
- ½ teaspoon ajwain seeds
- Pinch of bicarbonate of soda

1. In a bowl, add flour, chili powder, garlic powder, bicarbonate of soda, ajwain seeds, and salt.
2. Mix well.
3. Add enough water to make a smooth batter.
4. Dip boiled baby corn into the batter to coat.
5. Preheat your air fryer to 180°C (350°F).
6. Line the air fryer basket with foil and place the baby corns on the foil.
7. Cook baby corns for 10 minutes or until golden brown and crispy.

Salt and Pepper Baked Potatoes

Prep time: 5 minutes | Cook time:40 minutes |Serves 4

- 1 to 2 tablespoons olive oil
- 4 medium baking potatoes (about 9 to 10 ounces each)
- salt and coarsely ground black pepper
- butter, soured cream, chopped fresh chives, spring onions or bacon bits (optional)

1. Preheat the air fryer to 200°C/400°F.
2. Rub the olive oil all over the potatoes and season them generously with salt and coarsely ground black pepper. Pierce all sides of the potatoes several times with the tines of a fork.
3. Air-fry for 40 minutes, turning the potatoes over halfway through the cooking time.
4. Serve the potatoes, split open with butter, soured cream, fresh chives, spring onions or bacon bits.

Teff Veggie Burgers

Prep time: 20 minutes | Cook time:40 minutes |Serves 6

- 2 cups (473 ml) water
- ⅔ cup (168 g) brown teff grain
- 1 tbsp (15 ml) olive oil (*or use water sauté)
- 1 cup (142 g) minced onion
- 1 cup (78 g) minced mushrooms
- 1 medium carrot (61 g), grated
- 2 cloves (6 g) minced garlic
- 1½ tsp (3 g) salt
- ¼ tsp black pepper
- 1 (15.5-oz [439-g]) can kidney beans, drained and rinsed (or 1½ cups [439 g] homemade)
- ¼ cup (27 g) nutritional yeast

1. Bring the 2 cups (473 ml) of water to boil in a saucepan with a cover. Once it boils, stir in the teff, reduce to a simmer, cover and cook 15 to 20 minutes until the teff is cooked.
2. Heat the oil (*or water) in a large sauté pan over medium heat. Once hot, add the onion and sauté until translucent. Stir in the mushrooms, carrots, garlic, salt and pepper. Cook until the mushrooms have released all their liquid, the carrots are tender and the sauté mixture is dry.
3. Add the drained kidney beans to a mixing bowl and mash with a potato masher until all of the beans are broken up. Add in the cooked teff. It will be clumped up, but mash it in with the potato masher just like you did for the beans. Mix in the sautéed veggies and nutritional yeast. Divide the mixture into 8 balls. Flatten the balls into patties and place 2 to 4 in your air fryer, depending on its size.
4. Set your air fryer to 330°F (166°C). Cook 10 minutes on one side, until they are solid enough to easily flip. Then flip and cook on the other side until they are no longer mushy in the middle, about 10 minutes more.

Crispy Coconut Tofu Nuggets

Prep time: 10 minutes | Cook time:15 minutes |Serves 4

- ½ cup (56 g) white whole wheat flour (*or brown rice flour)
- 1 cup (240 ml) canned coconut milk
- 2 tsp (20 ml) soy sauce (*use gluten-free soy sauce or coconut aminos)
- 1 cup (80 g) finely shredded coconut
- ¾ cup (47 g) panko breadcrumbs
- 1 (14-oz [397-g]) package extra-firm or super-firm tofu (or firm tofu, pressed), cut into cubes

1. Sweet Thai chili garlic sauce for dipping
2. Mix the flour, coconut milk and soy sauce in a bowl.
3. Next, mix the coconut and panko in a second shallow dish.
4. Dip the tofu cubes in the wet batter, then put into the dry. You will need to press the dry on with your hand firmly. Then place on the bottom of your air fryer basket. Repeat until all the tofu is coated.
5. Preheat your air fryer to 390°F (199°C) unless your model doesn't require it. Once it's hot, carefully add the coconut tofu to your air fryer basket.
6. Set the cooking time to 5 minutes, and when the time is up, check to see how brown it is. Depending on your air fryer size, you will cook for an additional 3 to 5 minutes.
7. Repeat until all the tofu is cooked. How many times that takes will depend on the size of your air fryer. Serve with the chili garlic sauce.

Roasted Brussels Sprouts with Bacon

Prep time: 5 minutes | Cook time:25 minutes |Serves 4

- 4 slices thick-cut bacon, chopped (about 115g)
- 450g Brussels sprouts, halved (or quartered if large)
- freshly ground black pepper

1. Pre-heat the air fryer to 190°C.
2. Air-fry the bacon for 5 minutes, shaking the basket once or twice during the cooking time.
3. Add the Brussels sprouts to the basket and drizzle a little bacon fat from the bottom of the air fryer drawer into the basket. Toss the sprouts to coat with the bacon fat. Air-fry for an additional 15 minutes, or until the Brussels sprouts are tender to a knifepoint.
4. Season with freshly ground black pepper.

Steak Fries

Prep time: 5 minutes | Cook time:18 to 20 minutes |Serves 4

- 2 russet potatoes, scrubbed and cut into wedges lengthwise
- 1 tablespoon olive oil
- 2 teaspoons seasoning salt
- For the Seasoning Salt:
- 1 tablespoon kosher salt
- 2 teaspoons garlic powder
- 1 teaspoon paprika
- 1/2 teaspoon black pepper
- Instructions:

1. Pre-heat the air fryer to 200°C.
2. Toss the potatoes with the olive oil and the seasoning salt.
3. Air-fry for 18 to 20 minutes (depending on the size of the wedges), turning the potatoes over gently a few times throughout the cooking process to brown and cook them evenly.

FOR THE SEASONING SALT:

4. Mix all ingredients together in a small bowl.
5. Use as desired.

Spicy Sweet Potato Wedges

Prep time: 5 minutes | Cook time: 20 minutes | Serves 2

- 2 large sweet potatoes, cut into wedges
- Salt and pepper to taste
- 1 tablespoon red chili flakes
- 1 teaspoon ground cumin
- 1 teaspoon mustard powder
- 1 teaspoon chili powder
- 1 tablespoon rapeseed oil

1. Preheat air fryer to 180°C/350°F/Gas Mark 4.
2. In a mixing bowl, combine sweet potato wedges, red chili flakes, cumin, mustard powder, chili powder, and rapeseed oil. Stir well.
3. Transfer the sweet potato wedges into the air fryer basket and cook for 20 minutes.
4. Remember to shake the basket every 5 minutes to ensure even cooking.

Honey Roasted Carrots

Prep time: 5 minutes | Cook time: 12 minutes | Serves 2

- 1 tablespoon honey
- Salt and pepper to taste
- 450g baby carrots
- 1 tablespoon olive oil

1. In a mixing bowl, combine carrots, honey, and olive oil.
2. Season with salt and pepper.
3. Cook in air fryer at 200°C (390°F) for 12-minutes.

Charred Corn Salsa
Prep time: 10 minutes | Cook time:8 minutes |Serves 3

- 400g frozen corn kernels
- 1/2 cup finely chopped bell pepper (any color)
- 1/2 cup finely chopped red onion
- 1 garlic clove, finely chopped
- 1 tbsp olive oil
- 1 tsp kosher salt
- 3 tbsp chopped pickled jalapeños
- 1/2 cup roughly chopped fresh cilantro
- Tortilla chips

1. Preheat the air fryer to 200°C.
2. In a medium bowl, combine the corn, bell pepper, onion, garlic, olive oil, and salt.
3. Place the mixture in the air fryer basket and cook until the vegetables begin to char, about 6 to 8 minutes.
4. Transfer the salsa to a large bowl and mix in the jalapeños and cilantro. Serve immediately with the tortilla chips.

Easy Air Fry Seitan Riblets
Prep time: 20 minutes | Cook time:30 minutes |Serves 6

- 1 cup (120 g) vital wheat gluten
- ¼ cup (27 g) nutritional yeast
- 1 tsp (2 g) mushroom powder or vegan Worcestershire sauce
- 1 tsp (2 g) onion powder
- 1 tsp (2 g) salt (optional)
- ½ tsp garlic powder
- ¾ cup (177 ml) water or unsalted vegetable broth
- ¼ cup (60 ml) BBQ sauce

1. Add the vital wheat gluten, nutritional yeast, mushroom powder (or vegan Worcestershire sauce), onion powder, salt and garlic powder to your food processor.
2. Pulse until mixed well. Let the flour settle, then drizzle the water in through the top opening while you have the processor on.
3. Then let the food processor run for about 3 minutes more to knead the seitan. Remove the dough and put it on a cutting board and knead a little bit more with your hands.
4. Press and pull the dough into a circle that will fit into your air fryer basket. Then cut it in half so that it will cook a little faster and more evenly.
5. Place the 2 seitan pieces into your air fryer and cook on 370°F (188°C) for 8 minutes. Then flip the pieces over and cook 5 minutes more.
6. You could stop here and cut into chunks to use in stir-fries, slice thin for sandwiches or cut into pieces and pulse in your food processor to make ground seitan for tacos or spaghetti sauce.
7. Or go ahead and make riblets! Slice half of the seitan into ½-inch (12-mm) wide strips, then toss with about ¼ cup (60 ml) of your favorite BBQ sauce. Place in an oven-safe container that fits into your air fryer and cook at 370°F (188°C) for 5 minutes.

Spinach Samosa

Prep time: 5 minutes | Cook time: 15 minutes | Serves 2

- 225g almond flour
- 1/2 teaspoon baking soda
- 1 teaspoon garam masala
- 1 teaspoon coriander, chopped
- 40g green peas
- 1/2 teaspoon sesame seeds
- 40g potatoes, boiled, small chunks
- 2 tablespoons olive oil
- 175g boiled and blended spinach puree
- Salt and chilli powder to taste

1. In a bowl, mix baking soda, salt, and flour to make the dough.
2. Add 1 tablespoon of oil.
3. Add the spinach puree and mix until the dough is smooth.
4. Place in fridge for twenty-minutes.
5. In the pan add one tablespoon of oil, then add potatoes, peas and cook for 5-minutes.
6. Add the sesame seeds, garam masala, coriander, and stir.
7. Knead the dough and make the small ball using a rolling pin.
8. Form balls, make into cone shapes, which are then filled with stuffing that is not yet fully cooked.
9. Make sure flour sheets are well sealed.
10. Preheat air fryer to 200°C (390°F).
11. Place samosa in air fryer basket and cook for 10-minutes.

Cherry Bourbon BBQ Tofu or Cauliflower

Prep time: 5 minutes | Cook time:10 minutes |Serves 2

- 1 (15- to 20-oz [425- to 567-g]) block super-firm or high-protein tofu, cut into cubes (or firm tofu pressed overnight or *4 cups [500 g] cauliflower florets)
- A few spritzes of oil (**or use aquafaba)
- 2 tbsp (16 g) finely ground cornmeal
- ½ cup (120 ml) Cherry Bourbon BBQ Sauce

1. Add the tofu or cauliflower to a bowl and spritz with oil (or aquafaba). Sprinkle the cornmeal over the mixture and toss to lightly coat.
2. Preheat your air fryer to 390°F (199°C) unless your model doesn't require it. Once it's hot, add the coated tofu to your air fryer basket.
3. Set the cooking time to 5 minutes, and when the time is up shake or stir the tofu. Repeat for an additional 5 minutes.
4. Toss the cooked tofu or cauliflower in the Cherry Bourbon BBQ Sauce. Serve with roasted corn or your favorite sides

Air Fryer Asparagus

Prep time: 5 minutes | Cook time: 10 minutes | Serves 4

- 10 asparagus spears, woody ends removed
- Salt and pepper, to taste
- 1 garlic clove, minced
- 4 tablespoons of rapeseed oil

1. Preheat the air fryer to 200°C (400°F) for 5 minutes.
2. In a bowl, mix the garlic and rapeseed oil.
3. Coat the asparagus spears in the oil mixture and place them into the air fryer basket.
4. Season the asparagus with salt and pepper and cook for 10 minutes.

Vegan Mac and Cheese with a Surprise

Prep time: 15 minutes | Cook time: 25 minutes | Serves 4

- 1 cup (228 g) Savory Onion Cream, or substitute 1 cup (325 g) mashed cauliflower
- 3 tbsp (21 g) raw cashews, soaked overnight (or bring to a boil, remove from heat and let sit 15 minutes)
- ¼ cup (26 g) nutritional yeast
- ½ tsp granulated garlic powder
- ½ tsp smoked paprika
- ¼ tsp dry mustard powder
- ¼ tsp salt
- ⅛ tsp ground black pepper
- 2 cups (228 g) dry pasta, cooked according to the directions on the box (*use gluten-free)
- ¼ cup (28 g) panko breadcrumbs (*use gluten-free)

1. Place the Savory Onion Cream, cashews, nutritional yeast, garlic powder, smoked paprika, dry mustard powder, salt and black pepper into your blender and blend until smooth.
2. Pour the sauce on top of the cooked pasta and mix well. Get a nonstick pan that will fit in your size air fryer and either line with parchment paper or spray with a little oil. If you use parchment paper, cut the edges of the paper so it doesn't go over the top of the pan because it could burn on the heat element.
3. Add in the pasta mixture and top with the panko. Cover the pan with aluminum foil (or an oven-safe lid) and cook for 15 minutes on 350°F (177°C). Remove foil and cook 5 to 10 minutes more, until the panko is browned.

Air-Fried Seitan and Veggies with Peanut Sauce

Prep time: 10 minutes | Cook time: 20 minutes | Serves 4

- 4 cups (16 oz [453 g]) frozen broccoli, carrots and/ or cauliflower
- 2 cups (400 g) seitan, cut in chunks (*or use chickpeas or tofu) store-bought or see recipe
- ¾ cup (180 ml) water
- ½ cup (128 g) peanut butter
- 1 tbsp (15 ml) plus 2 tsp (10 ml) soy sauce (* and ** use coconut aminos)
- 2 tsp (10 ml) rice wine vinegar
- ¾ tsp ground ginger
- ¼ tsp granulated garlic
- Sriracha, to taste (optional)

1. Add the vegetables to your air fryer basket and cook for 350°F (177°C) for 10 minutes.
2. Shake the basket, add the seitan and cook 10 minutes more, or until the veggies are tender and the seitan begins to get a little crispy.
3. While the veggies and seitan are cooking, make the sauce by combining the water, peanut butter, soy sauce, vinegar, ginger, garlic and sriracha, if using, in a small mixing bowl. Whisk until smooth.
4. Serve the air fryer mixture over cooked rice, raw spinach or on its own. Just make sure it's smothered in peanut sauce because that's what makes this recipe amazing.

Appendix 1 Measurement Conversion Chart

Volume Equivalents (Dry)	
US STANDARD	**METRIC (APPROXIMATE)**
1/8 teaspoon	0.5 mL
1/4 teaspoon	1 mL
1/2 teaspoon	2 mL
3/4 teaspoon	4 mL
1 teaspoon	5 mL
1 tablespoon	15 mL
1/4 cup	59 mL
1/2 cup	118 mL
3/4 cup	177 mL
1 cup	235 mL
2 cups	475 mL
3 cups	700 mL
4 cups	1 L

Volume Equivalents (Liquid)		
US STANDARD	**US STANDARD (OUNCES)**	**METRIC (APPROXIMATE)**
2 tablespoons	1 fl.oz.	30 mL
1/4 cup	2 fl.oz.	60 mL
1/2 cup	4 fl.oz.	120 mL
1 cup	8 fl.oz.	240 mL
1 1/2 cup	12 fl.oz.	355 mL
2 cups or 1 pint	16 fl.oz.	475 mL
4 cups or 1 quart	32 fl.oz.	1 L
1 gallon	128 fl.oz.	4 L

Temperatures Equivalents	
FAHRENHEIT(F)	**CELSIUS(C) APPROXIMATE)**
225 °F	107 °C
250 °F	120 ° °C
275 °F	135 °C
300 °F	150 °C
325 °F	160 °C
350 °F	180 °C
375 °F	190 °C
400 °F	205 °C
425 °F	220 °C
450 °F	235 °C
475 °F	245 °C
500 °F	260 °C

Weight Equivalents	
US STANDARD	**METRIC (APPROXIMATE)**
1 ounce	28 g
2 ounces	57 g
5 ounces	142 g
10 ounces	284 g
15 ounces	425 g
16 ounces (1 pound)	455 g
1.5 pounds	680 g
2 pounds	907 g

Appendix 2 The Dirty Dozen and Clean Fifteen

The Environmental Working Group (EWG) is a nonprofit, nonpartisan organization dedicated to protecting human health and the environment Its mission is to empower people to live healthier lives in a healthier environment. This organization publishes an annual list of the twelve kinds of produce, in sequence, that have the highest amount of pesticide residue-the Dirty Dozen-as well as a list of the fifteen kinds ofproduce that have the least amount of pesticide residue-the Clean Fifteen.

THE DIRTY DOZEN	
The 2016 Dirty Dozen includes the following produce. These are considered among the year's most important produce to buy organic:	
Strawberries	Spinach
Apples	Tomatoes
Nectarines	Bell peppers
Peaches	Cherry tomatoes
Celery	Cucumbers
Grapes	Kale/collard greens
Cherries	Hot peppers

The Dirty Dozen list contains two additional itemskale/collard greens and hot peppers-because they tend to contain trace levels of highly hazardous pesticides.

THE CLEAN FIFTEEN	
The least critical to buy organically are the Clean Fifteen list. The following are on the 2016 list:	
Avocados	Papayas
Corn	Kiw
Pineapples	Eggplant
Cabbage	Honeydew
Sweet peas	Grapefruit
Onions	Cantaloupe
Asparagus	Cauliflower
Mangos	

Some of the sweet corn sold in the United States are made from genetically engineered (GE) seedstock. Buy organic varieties of these crops to avoid GE produce.

Appendix 3 Index

TESSA D. MILLER

Printed in Great Britain
by Amazon